Also by Wolfgang Schivelbusch

The Culture of Defeat
The Railway Journey
Disenchanted Night
Tastes of Paradise

THREE NEW DEALS

THREE NEW DEALS

Reflections on Roosevelt's America,
Mussolini's Italy, and Hitler's Germany,
1933–1939

WOLFGANG SCHIVELBUSCH

Translated by Jefferson Chase

METROPOLITAN BOOKS
HENRY HOLT AND COMPANY • NEW YORK

Metropolitan Books
Henry Holt and Company, LLC
Publishers since 1866
175 Fifth Avenue
New York, New York 10010
www.henryholt.com

Library of Congress Cataloging-in-Publication data
Schivelbusch, Wolfgang, 1941–
Three new deals: Reflections on Roosevelt's America, Mussolini's Italy,
and Hitler's Germany, 1933–1939 / Wolfgang Schivelbusch.—1st ed.
          p.   cm.
Includes bibliographical references and index.
ISBN-13: 978-0-8050-7452-9
ISBN-10: 0-8050-7452-X
1. New Deal, 1933–1939. 2. United States—Economic policy—1933–1945.
3. United States—Politics and government—1933–1945. 4. Italy—
Economic policy. 5. Italy—Politics and government—1933–1945.
6. Germany—Economic policy—1933–1945. 7. Germany—Politics
and government—1933–1945. I. Title

HC106.3.S3246 2006
330.9'043—dc22   2006044947

Henry Holt books are available for special promotions
and premiums. For details contact: Director, Special Markets.

First Edition 2006

Designed by Victoria Hartman

Printed in the United States of America
1   3   5   7   9   10   8   6   4   2

As force is always on the side of the governed,
the governors have nothing to support them but opinion.
It is, therefore, on opinion that government is founded;
and this maxim extends to the most despotic and the most military
governments as well as to the most free and popular.

—David Hume

Contents

THREE NEW DEALS

INTRODUCTION:
ON COMPARISONS

In September 1946, Sigfried Giedion, probably the most renowned historian of modern architecture, gave a lecture before the Royal Institute of British Architects in London. The editors of the *Architectural Review* were so taken with Giedion's ideas that they convened a symposium to discuss them, inviting such leading architects and architectural historians as Walter Gropius, Henry-Russell Hitchcock, Gregor Paulsson, William Holford, Lucio Costa, and Alfred Roth, as well as Giedion himself. The symposium took for its title that of Gideon's original lecture: "The Need for a New Monumentality."

For the first time in the history of modern architecture, the discipline was subjecting itself to fundamental self-criticism. The chief insight to emerge was that modernists, in their struggle against the historicism of the nineteenth century, had perhaps focused too exclusively on architecture's technical, functional side, to the exclusion of the complex set of desires and expectations that transcends everyday utility and distinguishes architecture from mechanics or engineering. "The people," wrote Giedion, "want buildings representing their social, ceremonial, and community life. They want their buildings to be more than a functional fulfillment. They seek the expression of their aspiration for joy, for luxury, and for excitement. Monumentality consists in the eternal need of the people to create symbols that reveal their inner life, their actions, and their social conceptions. . . . This demand for monumentality cannot, in the long run, be suppressed."[1]

Most of the participants agreed that they should have been more receptive to such expectations in the years before World War II. In the wake of World War I, modern architects had aspired to provide structural expressions of social revolution to the masses, by and for whom it had been carried out. But the masses had never understood—much less liked—modern architecture. And during the Great Depression, capitalism's period of crisis, they were drawn to modernism's bitterest enemies, National Socialism and Fascism, because these offered them something they wanted and needed, something that modernism had refused to provide them: monumentality.

The conflation of monumental—that is, backward-looking, neoclassical—architecture with the Third Reich and the other totalitarian regimes of the twentieth century reflects the political and ideological oppositions of the 1920s and '30s—as does the association of modern architecture with liberal democracy and the social-welfare state. The underlying assumptions entailed therein remained unquestioned into the 1970s. Even as late as the 1990s Bruno Zevi, the Italian patriarch of modern architecture, expressed "disgust" and "contempt" for an academic conference devoted to 1930s—read: Fascist/totalitarian—neoclassicism. In an article in the leading Italian architecture journal, *L'architettura*, he accused the organizers of "obfuscation, ignorance, arrogance, and idiocy," adding that the conference didn't deserve to be taken seriously because it promoted "excrement, shit, vomit, and spew."[2]

For decades critics ignored, or chose to ignore, the fact that neither Italian Fascism nor early Soviet Communism fit the paradigm. They also disregarded the affinities many leading practitioners of the modernist New Architecture movement in Germany—including Mies van der Rohe—had felt with Fascism during the initial years of the Third Reich. It took an entire generation after World War II before scholars, as part of a general effort to locate Nazism within a wider historical context, came to today's consensus that the earlier equations were too simplistic. Suddenly they woke up to the fact that neoclassical, monumental buildings had been constructed in Washington, Paris, London, and Geneva during the 1930s, just as they had in Berlin, Moscow, and Rome. They recognized that Mussolini's program of architectural functionalism, or "rationalism," was nothing other than an extension of modernism and that even the Third Reich, the great exemplar of antimodern philistinism, had taken a modernist approach when dealing with function rather than representation. They acknowledged that there had been architecturally modern Fascists and architecturally traditional liberals and that 1930s neoclassical monumentalism was just as widespread as the modernism that the Museum of Modern Art had dubbed the International Style in 1932. Instead of reducing neoclassicism to a side effect of totalitarianism, scholars became more interested in how various national, political, and ideological systems applied what Giorgio Ciucci calls "the specific aesthetics of power."[3] Architectural historian Louis Craig's term "government international" sums up this style well, as does Franco Borsi's assertion that "monumental architecture could signify equally the strength of the institutions in the democracies and the aggressive power of the state in the dictatorships."[4]

Critics began to ask why a majority of democratic nations in 1927 rejected modernist designs for the headquarters of the League of Nations, choosing instead a neoclassical, monumental one, why the Third Republic in France built the neoclassical Palais de Chaillot for the 1937 World's Fair, and why the architecture of Washington, D.C., received a monumentalist infusion under Roosevelt's New Deal. The answers were the same. Scholars gradually recognized neoclassical monumentalism—whether of the 1930s, the Renaissance, the French Revolution, or the Napoleonic empire—for what it is: *the* architectural style in which the state visually manifests power and authority. Although neoclassicism temporarily lost its hold with the rise of nineteenth-century liberal capitalism, in which the state restricted itself to a supervisory role and allowed the private sector to determine architectural aesthetics, it regained it in the twentieth century, beginning with increased state regulation of the economy in the years before World War I, continuing through the state's mobilization of the economy during the war, and culminating with its near-total intervention during the Depression.* The various state solutions to that crisis amounted to a defeat for liberal capitalism and a triumph for governmental authority.

Both the revolutionary states of Bolshevism and Fascism, as well as the reformist ones of the capitalist democracies, needed an architecture that would tower on behalf of, but also above, the people like a temple, inspiring trust, respect, and a quasi-religious sense of deeper meaning and community—while at the same time showing the rest of the world who it was dealing with. A concrete embodiment of the competition between political systems was the constellation formed by the three most spectacular buildings at the 1937 World's Fair in Paris. The monumental Palais de Chaillot, for which the government of the Third Republic had torn down the old Trocadéro, was strategically placed at the end of the central axis, flanked by the "massive pavilions" of the Soviet Union and Nazi Germany. The Palais symbolized France's self-perception as a major power, unwilling to back down before the two dictatorships, or rather, firmly holding center stage while shunting its rivals off to the sides.[5]

The primary sites for monumental construction and self-representation in the 1930s were capitals. Paris had already undergone a major monumental reconstruction under Georges-Eugène Haussmann in the 1860s and could thus be left rela-

---

*Whenever the term "liberal" or one of its derivatives is used in this book, it is not in today's American vernacular meaning of progressive, enlightened, emancipatory, and social-democratic, but in the traditional meaning still alive and valid in the 1930s. That is, the economic and political laissez-faire philosophy originating with Adam Smith and culminating in nineteenth-century Manchester capitalism. Along the same lines, "post-liberal" refers to political and economic arrangements in which the state plays an active role in directing and regulating the society.

The monumental facade of the Palais de Chaillot

tively untouched. But in Germany, the Soviet Union, and Italy, the regimes planned Haussmannesque transformations of Berlin, Moscow, and Rome. With varying degrees of radicalism, roads were constructed and expanded, and urban thoroughfares were laid out in widths previously reserved for city squares. Quaint old buildings, derided by Mussolini as "picturesque garbage," were torn down to make room for colossi such as the Hall of the People in Nazi Berlin and the Soviet Palace in Moscow, which aimed to set new records for height and volume.[6] (The Soviet Palace, for instance, was to stand over 1,345 feet tall, crowned by a 229-foot statue of Lenin.) Finally, city planners implemented state measures concerning traffic and hygiene suggested by prominent Sovietophile architects such as Corbusier, Gropius, and Ernst May. These were "plans of war," as Lazar Kaganovich, the man Stalin put in charge of the redevelopment of Moscow, characterized the Soviet General Plan of 1935.[7] The enemy that was to be eradicated was the laissez-faire architectural legacy of nineteenth-century liberalism, an unplanned jumble of styles and structures.

Not every regime pursued this struggle with the same resolve, and nowhere was total victory achieved. Fascism made the least progress toward its stated goal—assuming it was meant seriously—of tearing down much of Rome's medieval, Renaissance, and Baroque architecture and uncovering the antique city, which would then be blended in with new monumental structures.[8] Adolf Hitler and Albert Speer's attempt to replace Berlin with a new Nazi capital called Germania was hardly more successful, largely because military defeat interrupted construction before it could truly get under way. It was Stalinism that best succeeded in giving the national capital the desired face-lift. But even in Moscow, the state's most ambitious project, the Soviet Palace, was never realized.

Washington, D.C., saw a similar rash of construction projects. Most of the large-scale neoclassical buildings associated with the city of today were built between 1933 and 1939. They include the Federal Triangle, the National Gallery, the National Archives, the Supreme Court Building, various departmental and other government buildings, the Smithsonian Museum complex, and the Jefferson Memorial. In contrast to concurrent activity in Berlin, Rome, and Moscow, and to Haussmann's remodeling of Paris seventy years earlier, the basic layout of the city remained unchanged, and no historical buildings were demolished. For more than a hundred years, Washington had remained an impressive network of streets with a small village attached. What took place in the 1930s, then, was neither a war against the existing city nor a renewal based on the destruction of a previous urban layer but the architectural closing of empty spaces that had long been reserved for the construction of the capital.

The work undertaken between 1933 and 1939 explicitly harkened back to a plan for Washington conceived in 1902; that plan in turn was based on one drawn up in 1791 at George Washington's behest by architect Pierre Charles L'Enfant, who had fought with the Continental Army in the Revolutionary War. Raised at Versailles, L'Enfant brought to the job his childhood impressions of the Baroque palace gardens with their broad avenues and their interplay of straight, curved, and diagonal lines, which yielded an impressive variety of perspectives. Architectural historian John W. Reps has described it as a "supreme irony" that an architectural style "originally conceived to magnify the glories of despotic kings and emperors came to be applied as a national symbol of a country whose philosophical basis was so firmly rooted in democratic equality."[9]

It is no less ironic that the Baroque monumentality L'Enfant imported from Europe to America allowed the city of Washington to make the transition to the twentieth century with far less destruction than in the European capitals. The vision for Washington essentially took a giant leap from pre- to post-liberal monumentalism. Daniel Burnham, the man behind the 1902 plan,[10] summed up his philosophy in a curt imperative worthy of any of Hitler, Mussolini, or Stalin's urban developers: "Make no little plans, they have no power to stir men's souls."[11]

*   *   *

THERE ARE TWO lessons to be derived from the history of 1930s monumental architecture and its varying reception in the decades after 1945. The first shows how the same stylistic, formal, and technological developments—within architecture and elsewhere—can be used to serve radically different political systems. The second lesson demonstrates how poorly later generations are able to distinguish between form and content, especially when the object of historical study, as is the case with a defeated dictatorship, elicits general condemnation. Little has changed since Hegel's complaint about the flaw in "abstract thinking": that it cannot conceive of a handsome murderer.

Around the time that simplistic equations of monumentalism and totalitarianism fell out of fashion, historical research took a new direction. Fascism, National Socialism, and Stalinism were no longer seen as examples of sheer evil, and the complexities of their economic, social, psychological, and cultural structures came in for closer examination. Scholars discovered that Fascism and Nazism possessed, alongside their repressive and murderous tendencies, a social-egalitarian component and that the mass popularity of both regimes in the 1930s was due more to the latter than to the former. This scholarly recognition of the "socialist" side of National Socialism, as well as the engagement with Nazism's belief that its racial doctrine entailed the promise of equality for all members of the German people, or *Volk*, seemed shocking only because that side of Nazism had been so fully suppressed after 1945.

Much the same process—in reverse—was evident in reevaluations of U.S. history. The New Deal, idealized as the heroic benevolent alternative to the regimes in Germany and Italy, began to attract some criticism. Once historians were willing to consider the multiple components of National Socialism and Fascism, instead of merely categorizing both as "totalitarian," they also began to look beyond the simplistic dichotomy of liberal democracy on the one hand and repressive dictatorship on the other. This new scholarly direction tended to dispatch the legend of Roosevelt as infallible statesman and invited discussion of the New Deal as a series of economic misadventures, achieved through the force of mass propaganda and owing its success solely to America's victory in World War II. Still, these revisionist efforts to place the New Deal, Fascism, and National Socialism in a more differentiated historical context had little impact: in all three cases, the ideologically inspired visions of the past held sway.

The existence of this more nuanced approach could have opened up possibilities for investigating the points of convergence between Fascist Italy, Nazi Germany, and the deromanticized New Deal. But only on the margins did historians risk these comparisons. In the 1970s there were occasional forays in this direction among American and German historians, and in the 1980s among a small school of Italian academics interested in comparing Fascism and the New Deal.[12] John A. Garraty, a newcomer to the topics of both the New Deal and Nazism, published an article in 1973 comparing Roosevelt's programs and certain aspects of American political culture during his administration with those of the Third Reich. The affinities Garraty suggested were these: a strong leader; an ideology stressing the nation, the people, and the land; state control of economic and social affairs; and, finally, the quality and quantity of government propaganda. Garraty was careful to stress the obvious: that to compare is not the same as to equate. America during Roosevelt's New Deal did not become a one-party state; it had no secret police, the Constitution remained in force, and there were no concentrations camps; the New Deal preserved the institutions of the liberal-democratic system that National Socialism abolished.[13] For all his careful distinctions, however, Garraty's article, published in a major American historical journal, found little echo. The scent of sulfur surrounding Hitler and Mussolini was still too strong for historians to approach the facts directly and compare them.

CRITICS IN THE 1930s did not have the scruples we have today: of course, they had no way of knowing the genocidal course history would take. They were much more susceptible to the appeal of movements that offered protection—even false protection—against chaos than they were positively attracted to democracy. Or to put it another way, the defining historical moment for the mind of the 1930s was not the future defeat of Nazism in 1945 but the Great Depression in 1929. In the wake of global economic disaster, there was no particular reason to prefer the political system most closely associated with capitalism—liberal democracy—to new systems that promised a brighter future. On the contrary, people were more inclined to ask themselves whether democracy was inevitably doomed by the economic breakdown of liberal capitalism.

Indeed, the ideas discussed in Europe's remaining democracies show how willing many people within the liberal camp were to try to save the situation by jettisoning liberal ballast. Some suggested reintroducing state-directed economies like those during World War I; others proposed imitating various Fascist models. In 1933 Harold Macmillan, the conservative MP and later British prime minister, advocated a broad program of economic reforms that he described as "orderly capitalism." Critics argued, not without merit, that such ideas amounted to corporatism, the political system adopted by Italian Fascism.[14]

Europe's democratic left was affected even more profoundly than its liberal center by Nazism's rise to power in Germany. While the leaders of Europe's socialist parties were content merely to wring their hands over Hitler's success, refusing to acknowledge any failings on their own part, the younger party members and intellectuals were harshly self-critical. The most vocal anti-Fascists among the socialists were also those who called for socialism to learn from Fascism and National Socialism. Men like Stafford Cripps in England, Marcel Déat and Barthélémy Montagnon in France, and Henri de Man in Belgium were united in their contempt for the ossified party apparatus, which they saw as having robbed socialism of its spirit and strength. To their minds, it was no wonder that the masses that had once rallied behind socialism had been won over by Fascism. Not only had Fascism co-opted socialism's youthful vitality, sense of purpose, and readiness for conflict and sacrifice, it had also united its followers in mass movements whose appeal extended beyond the proletariat.[15] As the socialist dissidents saw it, the task now was to retake from Fascism what Fascism had taken from socialism, or as one might say, to conclude the cycle of borrowing begun by Mussolini when he, the once ardent socialist, created Fascism as his new form of socialism.[16]

* * *

THE SPECIFIC LESSON to be learned from Fascism and National Socialism was that it was possible to create a kind of national, non-class-specific socialism. Marcel Déat envisioned "a form of society that was not yet socialist but no longer capitalist," organized into a strong centralized state that controlled capital without appropriating it.[17] John Middleton Murry, one of the most prominent internal critics of the British Labour Party, was optimistic on the question of whether change would be democratic or dictatorial:

> A government of national security, which achieves the goal of economic separation of property and control, is just as compatible with the preservation of the democratic "form" as fascist social transformation is with the conservation of political freedoms.

Like many of his contemporaries in the early 1930s, Murry did not see Fascism as a system that necessarily included repression and terror. For the unorthodox minority of the left, Fascism was an intermediary path between socialism and liberalism whose initial propensity toward violence—on the analogy of the French and Russian revolutions—could be explained as the birth pangs of a radical new movement.[18]

Commentators freely noted areas of convergence among the New Deal, Fascism, and National Socialism. All three were considered postliberal state-capitalist or state-socialist systems, more closely related to one another than to classic Anglo-French liberalism. Hitler, Mussolini, and Roosevelt were seen as examples of plebiscite-based leadership: autocrats who came to power via varying but thoroughly legal means. No one, of course, failed to recognize the differences between the mass political parties of Fascism and National Socialism, with their legions of paramilitary thugs and organized mechanisms of state repression, and the pluralistic conglomeration that was the New Deal administration. Yet both liberal and Fascist commentators identified a number of similarities between the socially oriented policies of the New Deal and Fascist ideas of collective consolidation. The consensus among political scientists and economists of the time was that the United States, under Roosevelt in the spring and summer of 1933, had, in a process of voluntary consolidation, transformed itself into a postliberal state.

This synchronicity ended with America's entry into World War II and the Allies' victory over Fascism and National Socialism. Memories of the New Deal's common roots with its enemies were repressed, and postwar America was free to enjoy a myth of immaculate conception when it came to the birth of the liberal-democratic welfare state. Roosevelt, no longer named in the same breath with Hitler, Mussolini, and Stalin, posthumously became the patron saint of liberal democracy in its triumphant struggle against the forces of evil.

LARGELY REPRESSED AS it has been, a comparative perspective on the New Deal, on the one hand, and the Fascist and National Socialist regimes, on the other, may now be ripe for reconsideration. Certainly it can begin to provide answers to some of the questions that have persisted in the postwar years: How did the New Deal manage to become so successful an alternative to the totalitarian regimes of the 1930s? And what accounts for the widespread allegiances these regimes inspired, at least initially? To what extent was the New Deal's effectiveness due to its ability to incorporate the very elements that rendered these regimes so popular—a new vision of the nation based on collectivism, on economic and social planning, and embodied both in a charismatic leader and in monumental public works? The features with which totalitarianism was later most closely identified—political pressure to conform, repression, state terrorizing of dissidents, secret police units, and concentration camps—were not the things that made these regimes desirable. The people were attracted by the feeling of being treated as equals instead of being ignored and by the sense that they no longer had to fend for themselves but, rather, could enjoy the protection, security, and solidarity afforded by the new classless community of the nation. The New Deal, Fascist Italy, and Nazi Germany all profited from the illusion of the nation as an egalitarian community whose members looked out for one another's welfare under the watchful eyes of a strong leader.

The intention here is not to suggest that the New Deal's vision of national and social collectivism rendered America a version of the Italian or German models. Such an argument would be as absurd as claiming that Fascism and National Socialism were in fact liberal-democratic, given their adoption of American methods of advertising and mass persuasion. To identify areas of commonality is not to argue for sameness. As Garrity enjoined, to compare is not to equate.

· 1 ·

KINSHIP?

If there was one peacetime year in the first half of the twentieth century that represented the nadir of the liberal-democratic system and the high point for the rival Fascist-totalitarian order, it was 1933. Of the Central European republics that were founded with such fanfare after World War I, most were by that point ruled by authoritarian dictators. (Czechoslovakia was the great exception.) Fascism was celebrating its eleventh year in power, and with the election of the National Socialists in Germany, liberal democracy suffered an epochal defeat in Europe's largest industrialized nation. In March 1933, as a kind of symbolic confirmation of this triumphant momentum, a Fascist International was founded.[1]

At the beginning of the same month, Franklin Delano Roosevelt was inaugurated as president of the United States— a milestone that was seen alternately as American democracy's

vigorous reaction to global political and economic developments and as its tacit surrender to them. The broad-ranging
powers granted to Roosevelt by Congress, before that body
went into recess, were unprecedented in times of peace.
Through this "delegation of powers," Congress had, in effect,
temporarily done away with itself as the legislative branch of
government. The only remaining check on the power of the
executive was the Supreme Court. In Germany, a similar
process allowed Hitler to assume legislative power after the
Reichstag burned down in a suspected case of arson on February 28, 1933. As in the United States, the judiciary remained—
for the short term, at least—independent. Germany's highest
court, in fact, acquitted four suspects, including Bulgarian
Communist Georgi Dimitroff, in the Reichstag fire. But this
was the swan song of German judicial autonomy.

The View from Europe

The National Socialists hailed the emergency relief measures
undertaken during Roosevelt's first hundred days in office
as fully consistent with their own revolutionary program.
On May 11, 1933, the main Nazi newspaper, the *Völkischer
Beobachter*, offered its commentary in an article with the
headline "Roosevelt's Dictatorial Recovery Measures." The
author wrote, "What has transpired in the United States
since President Roosevelt's inauguration is a clear signal of the
start of a new era in the United States as well." The tone on
January 17, 1934, was much the same: "We, too, as German

National Socialists are looking toward America. . . . Roosevelt is carrying out experiments and they are bold. We, too, fear only the possibility that they might fail." And on June 21, 1934, the paper drew its initial conclusion about the success of the New Deal: "Roosevelt has achieved everything humanly possible in light of his narrow, insufficient basis."

Just as National Socialism superseded the decadent "bureaucratic age" of the Weimar Republic, the *Völkischer Beobachter* opined, so the New Deal had replaced "the uninhibited frenzy of market speculation" of the American 1920s. The paper stressed "Roosevelt's adoption of National Socialist strains of thought in his economic and social policies," praising the president's style of leadership as being comparable to Hitler's own dictatorial *Führerprinzip*. "If not always in the same words," the paper wrote, "[Roosevelt], too, demands that collective good be put before individual self-interest. Many passages in his book *Looking Forward* could have been written by a National Socialist. In any case, one can assume that he feels considerable affinity with the National Socialist philosophy." The newspaper admitted that Roosevelt maintained what it called "the fictional appearance of democracy," but it also proclaimed that in the United States "the development toward an authoritarian state is under way." The author added, "The president's fundamental political course still contains democratic tendencies but is thoroughly inflected by a strong national socialism."[2]

Hitler himself told American ambassador William Dodd that he was "in accord with the President in the view that the virtue of duty, readiness for sacrifice, and discipline should dominate the entire people. These moral demands which the

President places before every individual citizen of the United States are also the quintessence of the German state philosophy, which finds its expression in the slogan 'The Public Weal Transcends the Interest of the Individual.'" Even as late as 1938, Dodd's successor, Hugh R. Wilson, reported back positively to Washington about his conversations with Hitler:

> Hitler then said that he had watched with interest the methods which you, Mr. President, have been attempting to adopt for the United States in facing some of the problems which were similar to the problems he had faced when he assumed office. I said that in my short stay in Germany I had already noticed the similarity of some of the economic problems with which you were attempting to grapple, and those which he had attacked, and in some cases solved. I added that you were very much interested in certain phases of the sociological effort, notably for the youth and workmen, which is being made in Germany, and that one of my first tasks would be to report to you on how these were being carried out.[3]

Moreover, it wasn't just Nazis who saw America's development under Roosevelt in this light. The nonparty press in Germany, which until 1936 was largely free to report on the United States as it saw fit, also characterized Roosevelt as a charismatic authoritarian leader and his administration's policies as that of a state-socialist, economic dictatorship. The non-Nazi press was less interested in drawing explicit comparisons with National Socialism, but Germany's leading liberal newspaper, the *Frankfurter Zeitung*, still counted Roosevelt "among the men who have understood the collective soul of their peoples and who, with their mesmerizing youthful energy and confidence, know how to inspire new faith and vitality in the masses, which otherwise swing wildly back and forth between hope and doubt." "Roosevelt," the paper concluded, "is a leader [*Führer*] and reformer of his people in a new phase of their communal life."[4]

ENGLISH AND FRENCH commentators painted a similar picture. They routinely depicted Roosevelt as a commander in chief in times of emergency akin to the Roman Republic's *dictator* or as a plebiscitary autocrat à la Mussolini. (Hitler was seldom invoked.) Frenchman Bernard Fay, a Roosevelt admirer, called him "a veritable dictator supported by the affection and enthusiasm of the masses."[5] Comparisons with Fascism were made easier by the fact that Mussolini's regime, unlike National Socialism, had been in power for a number of years. It had already undergone its initial phase of revolutionary violence and was accepted, despite its dictatorial posturing, by the Western democracies as a member of the international political establishment. Mussolini had achieved the status of a welcome bastion against Bolshevism—a position the Western democracies denied to the newly inaugurated Hitler. That's the only explanation for the international regard Fascism enjoyed from the 1920s until Mussolini's invasion of Ethiopia in 1935. In Western eyes, Mussolini was a legitimate world leader, the charismatic antithesis to Lenin whose regime offered an efficient first line of defense against Communism. In contrast, National Socialism—all of its anti-Bolshevist rhetoric notwithstanding—

Et tu, Roosevelt? *Morning Post*, London, 1933.

was considered perilously revolutionary and, in its communal component, even proto-Bolshevist.[6]

A further, more specific reason why, in 1933, the New Deal was often compared with Fascism was that with the help of a massive propaganda campaign, Italy had several years earlier begun the transition from a liberal free-market system to a state-run or corporatist one. In the 1930s, corporatism was increasingly regarded internationally as a perfectly comprehensible response to the collapse of the liberal, free-market economy—as was the policy of national self-sufficiency practiced by the Stalinist Soviet Union in withdrawing from the world economy. Of course, the Italian corporatist program—which historian Maurizio Vaudagna calls "Fascism's most original innovation up to that point"—seemed infinitely preferable to the Communist "great leap forward" because it didn't involve the expropriation of private property.[7] There was hardly a commentator who failed to see elements of Italian corporatism in Roosevelt's managed economy under the National Recovery Administration, the institution formed in 1933 to maintain mandatory production and price "codes" for American industry. The Italian press was quite taken with these similarities, and Mussolini laid the groundwork for such comparisons in a book review he wrote of Roosevelt's *Looking Forward*. On the one hand, he identified a spiritual kinship:

> The appeal to the decisiveness and masculine sobriety of the nation's youth, with which Roosevelt here calls his readers to battle, is reminiscent of the ways and means by which Fascism awakened the Italian people.

In other passages, Mussolini was more reserved:

> The question is often asked in America and in Europe just how much "Fascism" the American President's program contains. We need to be careful about overgeneralizing. Reminiscent of Fascism is the principle that the state no longer leaves the economy to its own devices, having recognized that the welfare of the economy is identical with the welfare of the people. Without question, the mood accompanying this sea change resembles that of Fascism. More than that cannot be said at the moment.[8]

Mussolini's reserve reflected the customary etiquette among world leaders, who try to avoid appearing partisan: in July 1933, the month Mussolini's review appeared, his press department was ordered not to describe the New Deal as Fascist because it might provide welcome ammunition to Roosevelt's political enemies at home.[9] A year later, Mussolini was sufficiently convinced of the strength of the president's position to be rather less diplomatic in his choice of words. In his review of the Italian edition of *New Frontiers*, a book written by Roosevelt's secretary of agriculture, Henry A. Wallace, Mussolini wrote:

> The book as a whole is just as "corporativistic" as the individual solutions put forth in it. It is both a declaration of faith and an indictment of economic liberalism. . . . Wallace's answer to the question of what America wants is as follows: anything but a return to the free-market, i.e., anarchistic economy. Where is America headed? This book leaves no doubt that it is on the road to corporatism, the economic system of the current century.[10]

Mussolini's earlier edict notwithstanding, the Italian press also frequently drew comparisons between the United States and Italy, and the discussion was conducted in what historian Marco Sedda calls "a completely free climate."[11] There was unanimous agreement that the New Deal was just as antiliberal in its economic and social orientation as Fascism. In *Gerarchia* (Leadership), the Fascist Party's journal of political theory, Giovanni Selvi characterized the plans of the National Recovery Administration as "bearing a Fascist signature" and as "corporatism without the corporations."[12]

The main sticking point in such comparisons was that the New Deal, unlike Fascism, did not seek to do away with the democratic political system. One Fascist author tried to gloss over this difference by writing, "In the United States, too, capitalism has entered its corporatist phase." Another simply asserted that the postliberal economic order "connects the American movement with Fascism as well as all other social experiments that follow the Italian model." Other authors tried to gloss over the differences in political systems by narrowing their focus to Mussolini and Roosevelt's respective personalities, stressing that the American president's energy, strength of will, faith, and "modernity of vision establish him beyond doubt as one of the new type of statesmen."[13]

BEYOND WELCOMING THE postliberal economic elements of the New Deal, National Socialists and Fascists saw Roosevelt's election as a first-rate propaganda opportunity, insofar as they could claim that the world's most powerful nation was now heading in the same direction they had been pursuing and propagating for years. In one fell swoop, Fascism suddenly looked like a global force whose influence transcended national borders.

Yet this self-image was not without cognitive dissonance. Psychologically, the leaders of Italy and Germany were in a position similar to that of the owner of a not entirely reputable inn at which, to everyone's surprise, a rich gentleman has made a reservation. Were they supposed to feel pride and joy or a mixture of sympathy and contempt for the man who had come down so far in the world that he had no other place to go? Both reactions are apparent in the Italian and German discourse on the New Deal. In 1933, at least, developments in America gave only cause for satisfaction, with Nazis and Fascists seeing themselves confirmed by the most powerful nation on earth.

But by the middle of the decade, Germans and Italians began to divorce themselves from such notions.

The main reason for the change of heart was the cooling of relations between the liberal-democratic and Fascist nations after Italy's invasion of Ethiopia in 1935 and German-Italian involvement in the Spanish Civil War. In Western eyes, these were both examples of totalitarian expansionism. Italy and Germany shrugged off the anti-Fascist tone coming from Washington as the result of the New Deal's perceived economic failure. "The U.S.," opined one German periodical, "lacks the national unity and direct leadership that are the decisive preconditions for the success of bold policies, such as those Roosevelt initiated in 1933." The paper added that in contrast to the New Deal, "the National Socialist revolution has kept its promises."[14] The criticism had some factual basis. The jobless rate in the United States jumped significantly in 1937, almost reaching 1932 levels, while Germany and Italy both enjoyed full employment. If one accepts the consensus among historians today that the United States completely emerged from the Depression only with its entry into World War II, a further parallel appears between Fascism/National Socialism and the New Deal. All three ideologies required rearmament and subsequent war to restore their national economies to full health.

The View from America

Perhaps not surprisingly, comparisons of the New Deal with totalitarian ideologies were part and parcel of the everyday

rhetoric of Roosevelt's domestic enemies. A Republican senator at the time described the National Recovery Administration (NRA) as having gone "too far in the Russian direction,"
while even a Democrat accused FDR of trying "to transplant
Hitlerism to every corner of this country." Herbert Hoover
called for open resistance to FDR's policies: "We must fight
again for a government founded on individual liberty and
opportunity that was the American vision. If we lose we will
continue down this New Deal road to some sort of personal
government based upon collectivist theories. Under these ideas
ours can become some sort of Fascist government."[15]

Such sentiments could, of course, be put down to the usual
partisan politics and intraparty rivalries, were it not for the fact
that they were echoed by intellectual observers of economics
and social policies who were otherwise Roosevelt allies. They,
too, saw a Fascist element at the core of the New Deal. Writing in the *Spectator*, liberal journalist Mauritz Hallgren noted:

> We in America are bound to depend more upon the
> State as the sole means of saving the capitalist system.
> Unattended by black-shirt armies or smug economic
> dictators—at least for the moment—we are being forced
> rapidly and definitely into Fascism. . . .

Elsewhere, he observed:

> I am certain that in this country it will come gradually,
> dressed up in democratic trappings so as not to offend
> people. But when it comes it will differ in no essential
> respect from the fascist regimes of Italy and Germany.
> This is Roosevelt's role—to keep people convinced that

the state capitalism now being set up is entirely democratic and constitutional.[16]

In the *North American Review*, Roger Shaw concurred:

> The New Dealers, strangely enough, have been employing Fascist means to gain liberal ends. The NRA with its code system, its regulatory economic clauses and some of its features of social amelioration, was plainly an American adaptation of the Italian corporate state in its mechanics. The New Deal philosophy resembles closely that of the British Labour Party, while its mechanism is borrowed from the BLP's Italian antithesis.[17]

From a somewhat more orthodox Marxist perspective, V. F. Calverton wrote in the *Modern Monthly:*

> The NRA, without assuming a Fascist guise, is doing part of the job that European Fascism has set out to accomplish: namely, the liquidation of the little man and the dissolution of small business as an economic force. Thus Franklin D. Roosevelt, elected by the forgotten men of America, becomes the father of an economic tactic that purposes by its very nature to make those forgotten men totally forgotten by rendering them extinct as a class. In so doing, he is achieving one of the same economic objectives that European Fascism is accomplishing by more drastic and desperate methods.[18]

In that same publication, the head of the American Socialist Party, Norman Thomas, opined:

> The similarities of the economics of the New Deal to the economics of Mussolini's corporative state or Hitler's

totalitarian state are both close and obvious. The "liberal" garb in which so far Roosevelt has clothed his regimentation does not alter the essential and is itself wearing thin.[19]

"We are trying out the economics of Fascism without having suffered all its social or political ravages," declared George Soule, the liberal editor of the *New Republic*, in his 1934 book *The Coming American Revolution*.[20] In the *Political Quarterly*, Oswald Garrison Villard spoke more hypothetically:

> No one can deny that the entire Roosevelt legislation has enormously enhanced the authority of the President, given him some dictatorial powers, and established precedents that would make it easy for any successor to Mr. Roosevelt, or for that gentleman himself, to carry us far along the road to fascism or state socialism.[21]

A 1934 article for *Harper's Magazine* by J. B. Mathews and R. E. Shallcross asked, "Must America Go Fascist?" The authors argued:

> It is in the very nature of planned recovery, its methods and its objectives, that we find the tendency which, if developed to its logical conclusion, arrives at the fascist stage of economic control. Mild measures have failed and by their failure have prepared the way for accentuating the tendency toward fascist control.[22]

In 1935, Gilbert H. Montague, in the *Annals of the American Academy of Political and Social Sciences*, had offered his conclusion: "The NRA matched a form of executive law making that was unconsciously but nevertheless essentially fascistic."[23]

By and large, then, American observers had the same picture as their European counterparts of the New Deal's kinship with Fascism. Both were seen as a form of postliberal style of government whose main thrust was toward social planning and a state-directed economy. At the same time, American commentators stressed the fundamental difference that the New Deal, unlike Fascism, had preserved individual civil liberties. That raised the question of whether the New Deal was America's answer to or a first sign of its infection by Fascism. In an article in the *New York Times*, Norman Thomas asked, "To what extent may we expect to have the economics of fascism without its politics?"[24]

The New Dealers themselves always tried to avoid, in public at least, giving the impression that their policies had anything to do with the autocratic and totalitarian systems of Europe. This is hardly surprising, since the greatest fear of American politicians during the 1930s was being labeled "un-American." But there were exceptions in which members of the administration acknowledged affinities. Roosevelt himself once spoke in the presence of journalists of Mussolini and Stalin as his "blood brothers." And during the public unveiling of the National Industrial Recovery Act, when Roosevelt referred to the industrial associations that had been reconstituted by the codes as "modern guilds," those fluent in the jargon may well have recognized the reference to the corporatist system associated with Fascism.[25]

In private, Roosevelt was much more frank about his sympathy for Mussolini and his interest in the Italian leader's economic and social order. In contrast to Hitler, with whom he

always felt a world of social, ideological, and political difference, Roosevelt had nothing but "sympathy and confidence" in
Mussolini up until the mid-1930s.[26] "I don't mind telling you in
confidence," FDR remarked to a White House correspondent,
"that I am keeping in fairly close touch with that admirable
Italian gentleman." One of Roosevelt's first acts after taking
office in March 1933 was to appoint Breckinridge Long,
ambassador to Rome. A longtime political ally, Long made no
secret of his enthusiasm for Fascism's social model. FDR had
Long report his impressions from Rome directly to him—not,
as was customary, via the State Department. In response to
Long's first enthusiastic missive, Roosevelt is quoted as saying,
"There seems to be no question that [Mussolini] is really interested in what we are doing and I am much interested and deeply
impressed by what he has accomplished and by his evidenced
honest purpose of restoring Italy."[27]

Much the same was true of those who worked closely with
the president. They, too, were careful not to publicly acknowledge either the convergence between what they doing in their
own country and Fascist models or the interest some of them
took in the Communist experiments in the Soviet Union. Pri-
vately, it was a different story. There may be no definitive proof
for the allegation that the head of the NRA, Hugh Johnson,
was so taken by a book about Italian corporatism that he often
gave it as a gift,[28] but there is considerable evidence that argues
for pro-Fascist affinities within the inner and outer circles of
the New Deal.

Rexford Tugwell, the man who was known as the most left-
wing member of Roosevelt's brain trust and who was frank

about his admiration for the Soviet planned economy, was also open in his respect for Mussolini's economic policies, though he otherwise rejected Fascism on ideological grounds. Returning from a fact-finding trip to Italy, Tugwell noted in his diary that in its efforts to overcome the economic crisis and modernize society, the Mussolini regime had done

> many of the things which seem to me necessary. And at any rate [Italy] is being rebuilt physically in a systematic way. Mussolini certainly has the same people opposed to him as F.D.R. has. But he has the press controlled so they cannot scream lies at him daily. And he has a compact and disciplined nation although it lacks resources. On the surface, at least, he seems to have made enormous progress.

He was also impressed by Fascism's ability to be a motor for change: "It's the cleanest, neatnest [*sic*], most efficiently operating piece of social machinery I've ever seen. It makes me envious."[29]

He was not alone in feeling jealous of the ease with which Mussolini seemed to have remade Italian society. Lorena Hickok, a close friend of Eleanor Roosevelt's and a journalist who covered stories related to the New Deal, wrote of a local government official complaining, "If Roosevelt were actually a dictator, we might get somewhere. This way it is hopeless." To which Hickok added, "I am almost forced to agree with him. If I were 20 years younger and weighed 75 pounds less, I think I'd start out to be the Joan of Arc of the Fascist Movement in the United States."[30]

*   *   *

AT NO POINT did either Adolf Hitler or National Socialism enjoy the mixture of respect and goodwill shown by the first Roosevelt administration toward Mussolini and his movement. Yet that did not prevent Washington from closely examining individual measures and programs undertaken in Berlin to see if they were suitable for emulation. Roosevelt's Secretary of the Interior, Harold Ickes, for instance, proclaimed, "What we are doing in this country were some of the things that were being done in Russia and even some things that were being done under Hitler in Germany. But we are doing them in an orderly way."[31]

To an extent, the difference in Washington's stance toward Italy and Germany reflects national clichés. Italy was the land of the operetta, incapable of posing any sort of serious threat. Germany represented precisely the opposite: America's great enemy in World War I, and one that had been demonized by propaganda and defeated only after tremendous effort. From its very inception, National Socialism appeared to be the apogee of Teutonic aggressiveness and barbarism. The propaganda image from World War I of German soldiers impaling Belgian babies on their bayonets merely had to be transferred to the anti-Jewish pogroms, and the air of innocence and harmlessness that Germany had projected during the fourteen years of the Weimar Republic was put to rest. Moreover, the Nazi revolution was just making itself felt, whereas by the early 1930s the street violence that had accompanied Mussolini's rise to power was a thing of the past. Liberal outrage at Fascist violence toward political enemies had long since waned, to be replaced by admiration for the newfound precision with which the Italian rail system kept to its schedules.

Common Ground

Beyond general assertions—or accusations—of commonalities, there was a particular theoretical basis for the open-mindedness of many American intellectuals toward Fascism: the philosophical school of pragmatism. Citing German historian Peter Vogt, one might speak of an "elective affinity" that pragmatists had for the European Fascists. Or as American historian John P. Diggins put it, "Fascism appealed, first of all, to the pragmatic ethic of experimentation."[32] In the 1920s, American intellectuals disheartened by the failures of liberalism let themselves be fooled into thinking that Fascism represented the realization of their ideals, much as intellectuals like Beatrice and Sidney Webb became infatuated with Stalinism a decade later, after their disillusionment with anemic Western socialism.

For our purposes, pragmatism may simply be considered turn-of-the-century America's philosophy of modernization. Having greatly influenced American Progressivism in the two decades before World War I, it proceeded from the assumption that classical enlightened rationalism and liberalism were no longer adequate for the economic and social conditions that had arisen by the end of the nineteenth century. Thus, a number of pragmatist political and social thinkers were prepared to use trans- or postliberal methods to modernize the economy, society, the state, and public morality. No one suggested that individual liberties—one of liberalism's main achievements—be eradicated. But there was a high degree of acceptance for comprehensive state control, planning, and direction, as long as the economic and social goal remained a "conscious, intelligent ordering of society." Those were the words of pragmatist philosopher Herbert W. Schneider, a disciple of John Dewey's, who taught at Columbia University. Schneider also described Thomas Jefferson's ideals of the American republic as "Jefferson's fascism."[33]

Pragmatist sympathizers viewed Fascism's emphasis on political repression as a regrettable but understandable secondary phenomenon. Historian Charles W. Beard, for example, wrote, "It would be a mistake to allow feelings aroused by contemplating the harsh deeds and extravagant assertions that have accompanied the Fascist process (as all other historical changes) to obscure the potentialities and lessons of the adventure."[34] On another occasion, Beard sought to distinguish Fascism from "terrible despotism" along the lines of czarist Russia, comparing it instead with the American system of checks and balances.[35]

IN THE PRAGMATIST vernacular, the word "Fascism" was more or less a synonym for state control. That connotation, current in the 1930s, explains why the term "economic Fascism" was commonly used to refer to the New Deal. From our perspective today, and with reference to the systems adopted by other European countries—such as Sweden, also in 1933—it might be more accurately described as social-democratic planning. The comparison with Fascism probably reflected the American tendency to perceive any limits on economic freedom as limits on freedom in general. Or possibly the idea of restricted economic freedom was made more palatable when it was characterized as Fascism as opposed to socialism or even social democracy. Whatever the reason, it is striking that observers at the time immediately deemed every form of state intervention in capitalism at least quasi-Fascist.

THERE WAS BROAD consensus in the 1930s that a "shirt movement" (a reference to Fascists' proclivity for uniforms) could not just be simply imported into the United States. In other words, to be successful, American "Fascism" had to take on American form. Or to cite a dictum usually attributed to Huey Long: "When America gets Fascism it will call it Anti-Fascism."[36]

There are a variety of explanations for why a homegrown American movement with Fascist affinities like the New Deal could succeed without resorting to repression and totalitarian control. One argument is that certain Fascist principles, including egalitarianism, conformity, and classlessness, which had to be imposed by force in Europe, had long been a reality in the United States—without, of course, being recognized as such. In a 1934 article titled "Is Fascism Possible in America?" Leon Samson wrote, "American democracy is proof against Fascism, not only because it is formally anti-fascist, but also because it contains and conceals elements that are fascist in substance and that serve to immunize American society to special fascist forms."[37]

Another theory is that America's transition from a liberal to a quasi-Fascist system was so gradual that people didn't notice it was taking place. Waldo Frank made that argument in his article "Will Fascism Come to America?," also from 1934:

The NRA is the beginning of American Fascism. But unlike Italy and Germany, democratic parliamentarianism has for generations been strong in the Anglo-Saxon world; it is a tribal institution. Therefore, a Fascism that disposes of it, rather than sharpens and exploits it, is not to be expected in North America or Britain. Fascism may be so gradual in the United States that most voters will not be aware of its existence. The true Fascist leaders will not be the present imitators of German Führer and Italian condottieri, prancing in silver shirts. They will be judicious, black-frocked gentlemen; graduates of the best universities; disciples of Nicholas Murray Butler and of Walter Lippmann.[38]

Contemporary observers' views on the preservation of political democracy were colored by their prior positions. Liberals simultaneously feared the demise of democracy—for example, through Roosevelt's attempts to gain influence over the Supreme Court—and celebrated the New Deal as a victory for democracy over dictatorship. Meanwhile, realists and cynics schooled in de Tocqueville's classic analysis of American democracy concluded, "Possibly there will be no need to curb democratic liberties; possibly enlightenment has discovered that suppression is far more dangerous than freedom."[39]

At the 1934 International Congress for Philosophy in Prague, Columbia University professor William Pepperell Montague—a colleague of Schneider's—coined the phrase "Fabian Fascism" for the New Deal—or, more precisely, for the further development of certain New Deal measures that he himself was proposing.[40] The phrase "Fabian Socialism" referred to the British, gentlemanly version of socialism or democratic socialism; "Fabian Fascism," therefore, suggested a civilized version of Fascism—Fascism with a human face. Yet Montague was less sanguine than many others about the possibility of avoiding the violence of European Fascist movements and of reforming America's liberal system "by democratic methods and in a spirit of goodwill . . . gently." His alternative was to suggest a "dual economy of fascistic communism and democratic capitalism." While preserving the rights of those who had jobs within the capitalist system, Montague's plan was to incorporate the unemployed into communes, "islands of refuge from that world of competition." The communes would, in turn, form an autonomous economic system of their own and be organized along dictatorial, technocratic lines. In the language of Montague's pragmatic recipe, that meant "capitalism for those who can afford it accompanied by communism for those who need it."

A significant difference between Montague's proposal and Fascism as it existed at the time was that the individual would retain the freedom of choice—for instance, he could sign up to submit to a communal dictatorship for as many as three years or opt "to get out of the system if he does not like it."

The idea of a dual economy was nothing foreign to the New Deal. Indeed, a dual economy was already operating in programs like the Subsistence Homesteads, the Civilian Conservation Corps, and the Tennessee Valley Authority.* In all of these initiatives, specific areas of economic and social life were exempted from the normal workings of liberal capitalism. The homestead

---

*The Civilian Conservation Corps, a job creation program for young men in the 1930s, has often been compared to similar programs in the Third Reich; the Subsistence Homesteads and the Tennessee Valley Authority will be discussed in detail in later chapters of this book.

program, for example, was organized along quasi-military lines that were hardly distinguishable from similar undertakings by Fascists and National Socialists.

MILITARY STRUCTURES AND metaphors constituted another link between the three systems. For both Fascism and National Socialism, war was an act of creation that determined everything that followed. Both saw World War I as the ultimate demise of liberalism. Post-1918 European democracy was, in their eyes, no more than an attempt to revive the deceased by applying makeup to the corpse. The war—or, more precisely, the front experience—had brought forth something new: a sense of community among those who fought, a conviction that they had been purified, hardened, and remade. The "fire" of the front had eradicated class divisions and forged a new sort of comradeship. Fascism and National Socialism saw themselves as the continuation of soldiers' solidarity, as heroic, messianic movements that would invigorate nations still ruled by outdated ideas with new revolutionary spirit. Politics was a call to arms on the home front.

Numerous features of these movements reflected the war experience: the principle of leadership, the reliance on uniforms, the storm troopers, the emphasis on all-or-nothing political struggle over debate, and the use of the word "battle" for every major economic enterprise. The rhetoric of "seizures of power" in both Italy and Germany recast what were, in fact, legal changes in government as the victorious end of the soldiers' long march home; as the reconquest of the nation from the rule of liberalism; as the displacement of merchants by warriors;

and as the reanimation of the spirit of national solidarity with which Germany and Italy had been infused when they declared war in 1914 and 1915 respectively. Even after the Mussolini and Hitler regimes solidified their hold on power, war mythology continued to inform the transformation of the liberal-parliamentary state into an autocracy patterned on military models.

The Fascists' fondness for bellicose metaphors is well known; less familiar is the role played in the New Deal by the rhetoric and psychology of war. The New Deal's hawkish self-conception has been obscured, except within the most specialist circles, by the mainstream view of World War II as a conflict waged as a last resort by the United States on behalf of peace and liberty against immoral aggressors bent on military conquest. Roosevelt's administration is seen as a government of benevolent, peace-loving businessmen who had no choice but to fight to combat rapacious totalitarian regimes and save the world from total militarization.

Roosevelt's inaugural address of 1933, however, reveals a rather different stance toward war and its relationship to mercantilism. In it, he blamed the "money changers" for the economic crisis, and he made it one of the first priorities of his administration to drive them from the temple of the nation. It was not enough to take economic and social steps against the Depression; one had to declare war on it. Without such a declaration, which united the nation in a life-or-death mission, there was no way of summoning energy for the necessary sacrifices. Today, the tone of Roosevelt's address is reminiscent of a rallying cry in conventional wartime propaganda:

If we are to go forward, we must move as a trained and loyal army willing to sacrifice for the good of a common discipline. We are, I know, ready and willing to submit our lives and property to such discipline, because it makes possible a leadership which aims at a larger good. I assume unhesitatingly the leadership of this great army of our people dedicated to a disciplined attack upon our common problems.

Moreover, Roosevelt had no scruples about invoking the possibility of imposing something like martial law, should the country fail to heed his call for solidarity:

I shall not evade the clear course of duty that will then confront me. I shall ask the Congress for the one remaining instrument to meet the crisis—broad executive power to wage a war against the emergency, as great as the power that would be given to me if we were in fact invaded by a foreign foe.[41]

In the spring of 1933, these words sounded less metaphoric than they do now because they reverberated with the memories of recent historical events. Like the proponents of Fascism and National Socialism, when the leaders of the New Deal talked about the experience of war, they were referring to World War I.

CALLS FOR A great display of national strength, akin to that required in wartime, had grown louder even before 1933 as people came to realize conventional economic and political means would not suffice to overcome the Depression. As early as 1931, Gerard Swope, the progressive-minded chairman of General Electric, unveiled a crisis-management plan replete with war analogies:

> If we were faced with war, the President would immediately call a special session of Congress to declare war and raise armies. This unemployment situation in many ways is more serious even than war. Therefore it is suggested that an extra session of Congress be called and the President request it to issue a billion dollars of bonds; and that then a campaign be organized to sell these bonds, much as the Liberty Bond campaigns were organized when we entered the war thirteen years ago.[42]

Swope wasn't the only one drawing war comparisons in 1931. In a book published that same year, Richard T. Ely, a leading Progressive economist, proposed forming an army of the unemployed, led by a general staff of economists, who "should go to work to relieve distress with all the vigor and resources of brawn and brain that we employed in the World War."[43]

These suggestions were anything but militaristic exceptions in an otherwise civil, pacifistic discourse. They were an expression of the crisis mood around 1930—understood and accepted by everyone, save men like Herbert Hoover, who as president rejected the Swope plan as "fascist and monopolistic." The war metaphor influenced nearly all of the New Deal's reform programs and the institutions put in place to implement them. The NRA was modeled on the War Industries Board of 1917, established by Woodrow Wilson to subordinate industry to the needs of wartime production, and it was directed by a former general who had served on that body. The Civilian Conservation Corps was paramilitary in structure. Even programs that seemed far removed from military purposes—the construction of settlements, the regulation of rivers, and the production of electricity—were thoroughly infused with the aura of wartime mobilization. Indeed, the Tennessee Valley Authority was presented to the public as a continuation of a defense project from World War I.

Extending the military metaphor, the New Deal could be seen as a veteran's reunion, reconvening the bureaucrats who had managed the wartime economy in 1917 and 1918. For them, the New Deal was an occasion to bring a chapter of history that had ended in disappointment, to a happier conclusion. Tugwell spoke for many when he said that the wartime economy had been a kind of socialism and regretfully added that with the war's end a great experiment had been broken off in midstream. Such sentiments were echoed in the nostalgic euphoria with which early Fascism and National Socialism pursued their experiments. Journalists who witnessed events on both sides of the Atlantic found the popular mood in the first days of the New Deal reminiscent of the Fascist March on Rome in 1922 and the German elections in March 1933.[44]

There is no way to understand the mentality, rhetoric, and symbolism of the New Deal without reference to World War I and the idea of a historical second chance—just as it is impossible to comprehend Fascism without taking into account the myth of the Front. Yet the roots of the metaphor and the psychology of war reach even deeper.

Liberators from Capital

During the two decades prior to World War I, Germany, Italy, and the United States saw the rise of reform and protest movements that focused on liberalism's failure to deal with the economic and social consequences of the modern age. Originally enlightened and progressive, liberalism seemed to have spent its vitality and devolved into an economic order that increasingly polarized society into rich and poor—and into a political system as obsolete for mass society at the end of the nineteenth century as feudal absolutism had been for the emerging bourgeois society a hundred years before. Much the same was true of liberal culture, which, it was felt, had ceased to serve the causes of enlightenment and emancipation, degenerating into an industry of distraction that worked to secure the rule of the few over the many. What disgusted the critical elites even more than economic inequality was the mass-production of cheap, manipulative popular culture. For the generation that was born around 1870 and reached adulthood in the 1890s, this commercialized culture was all the more intolerable because it ran contrary to the lofty ideal of the nation on which they had been raised, and which had driven the wars of national unification in all three countries. That ideal was rejected as society entered a period of uninhibited acquisitiveness. The Civil War in the United States was followed by the Gilded Age of the robber barons; German unification in 1871 by financial speculation and a series of stock market collapses; the founding of the Italian nation-state in 1870, by parliamentary corruption.

Those who considered themselves modern in 1890 were no longer liberals. Some turned to aestheticism. Others dedicated themselves to the task of saving nature from capitalist destruction or of reclaiming technology from the all-consuming demands of profit making. Others, still, sought an alternative to laissez-faire anarchy in social organization, discipline, and, ultimately, nationalism, which would seek to revive the idealism of the nation's formative years. One main leitmotif of the postliberal generation at the turn of the century was the idea of liberating the state from the businessmen, promoting it from the role of a mere night watchman working in the service of capital to one of a powerful director telling the moneymen what to do.

The postliberals' motives were seldom as selfless as they claimed. Once the final frontiers of laissez-faire capitalism, and the opportunities they afforded, had been closed, few paths remained for economic or social mobility. In contrast to the bourgeoisie of finance and industry, members of the middle class could only improve their standing through education or professional training. The need to find something to aspire to other than the liberal ideal of entrepreneurship produced a new career type: the administrator or technocrat. Lacking capital resources of their own, members of the new managerial class viewed themselves as the true elite, one whose technical and professional qualifications made them superior to the entrepreneurs and whose calling it was to direct the economy, society, and, ultimately, the entire nation.

*   *   *

POSTLIBERAL CONCEPTIONS OF a new economic, social, and state order drew on two main sources: the socialist theory of synthesis between the economy and the state and the Prussian model of state control of the economy. By the turn of the century, as parts of the middle classes came to adopt the concept of socialism, there were a number of novel syntheses. Abandoning the Marxist dogma of the proletariat, Christian, National, Prussian, and other socialisms offered doctrines of salvation for everyone, regardless of class.

The American equivalent of these movements was Progressivism, from which the New Deal drew many of its ideas; indeed, many of the New Deal's proponents began their careers as Progressives. The movement that had such a great effect on the young Franklin D. Roosevelt was heavily influenced by the Prussian-German model. In 1912, he cited German reformers as models for a new balance between individual freedom and collective responsibility: "They passed beyond the liberty of the individual to do as he pleased with his own property and found it was necessary to check this liberty for the benefit of the freedom of the whole people."[45] Moreover, all of the leading Progressive figures, including Woodrow Wilson, studied either in Germany or at American universities founded along German lines. In the process, they came to appreciate the Hegelian theory of a strong state and Prussian militarism as the most efficient way of organizing modern societies that could no longer be ruled by anarchic liberal principles.[46] This influence culminated in William James's famous essay "The Moral Equivalent of War" (1910), which stressed the central importance of discipline, order, and planning. Ironically, a few years later, American Progressives declared Prussian militarism to be the scourge of humanity, arguing that it was morally necessary for America to enter World War I in defense of freedom and democracy.[47]

The militarism of the American Progressives brings to mind Mussolini and his Italian Socialist faction, which saw World War I mainly as a means to world revolution. For the technocrats among the American Progressives, the country's entry into the war was more than a defense of democracy—it was their chance to take over the leadership of state. In a single step, they could, perhaps, achieve what the industrial magnates had always been able to obstruct in peacetime: the fundamental renewal of the economy, society, and the nation. In Progressive rhetoric, the words "warfare" and "welfare" soon became almost interchangeable.

Progressives maintained their lofty aspirations for the duration of the war. Under the aegis of "wartime socialism," the leadership of society and the economy was suddenly and seemingly miraculously entrusted to the hands of specialized managers who were now responsible not to the private owners of capital but to the nation itself. In their own view, that made them the only legitimate leaders of the American people. The euphoria of this period equaled that of the early days of the New Deal. A 1917 report by one wartime manager in Washington, D.C., could have been written in 1933:

> Enthusiasm for social service is epidemic. A luxuriant crop of new agencies is springing up. We scurry back and forth to the national capital; we stock offices with typewriters and new letterheads; we telephone feverishly, regardless of expense, and resort to all the devices of efficient "publicity work." It is all very exhilarating, stimulating, intoxicating.

The Progressive bureaucrats were driven by the conviction of entering a new enlightened age of "democratic collectivism." As one of them exulted, "*Laissez-faire* is dead. Long live social control: social control, not only to enable us to meet the rigorous demands of the war, but also as a foundation for the peace and brotherhood that is to come."[48]

· 2 ·

LEADERSHIP

Today, Adolf Hitler and Franklin Delano Roosevelt are seen as antipodes; indeed, it is hard to imagine a more dramatic study in human contrasts. Hitler is remembered as the plebeian parvenu, the hysterical demagogue, the unscrupulous dictator, the incarnation of barbarism, evil, and totalitarianism. Roosevelt is fondly recalled as the patrician gentleman, the self-confident leader blessed with innate personal and political authority, the very embodiment of liberal-democratic humanism. But contemporaries in the 1930s took a different view, as do some recent historical researchers. For them, Hitler and Roosevelt were both charismatic leaders who held the masses in their sway—and without this sort of leadership, neither National Socialism nor the New Deal would have been possible.

An important element of such charisma is the fact that the leader occupies a clear, symbolically potent position outside the established circles of power and their supporting institutions. The charismatic leader is a man who stands above party politics, whether he is someone who has risen from the anonymity of the masses or has broken ranks with the ruling class. Their backgrounds may have been radically different, but Hitler, the ordinary soldier from World War I, and Roosevelt, the privileged patrician, were both outsiders with enough distance from the "system" to fulfill the role of political messiah. An article in the French periodical *La revue mondiale* highlighted Roosevelt's aristocratic aura as a major element of his perceived charisma. One of the main reasons for Roosevelt's popularity, the article said, was that here "an aristocrat by blood, a patrician . . . took the side of the people, against the magnates of finance and industry."[1]

Charismatic leadership arises in crisis situations when the usual system of political representation no longer yields results or inspires public enthusiasm. In sociological terms, the phenomenon can be described as the direct plebiscitary connection between the masses and the leader, bypassing intermediary institutions like parliaments and parties, which have been discredited by the crisis. Psychologically, it can be seen as the convergence of the masses and the charismatic individual in mutual rebellion against the old system.

Acute observers between the wars immediately recognized that the period's totalitarian dictators differed from old-style despots, whose rule was based largely on the coercive force of their praetorian guards. The formula *la démocratie c'est la dictature* (and, equally, its inversion) succinctly expressed the insight that with the advent of mass society, the old notions of individual political liberty and faith in reason were hopelessly outmoded.

Roosevelt, the patrician, reaching out to the common man *(Cartoon by Clarence D. Batchelor, 1934)*

Charismatic leadership independent of any specific political system presupposed the ability on the part of the head of state to build and maintain a direct emotional connection with the masses—that is, to do on the national level and continuously what traditional politicians had been able to achieve only sporadically for a select constituency. In 1932 Belgian sociologist Henri de Man pointed out that the charismatic leader had to possess the fearlessness of a lion tamer. What he meant was not the leader's freedom from fear in dealing with the masses but, rather, his disregard of bourgeois caution—or in de Man's words, his "sovereign indifference to material concerns." The phrase underscores the risk-taking, adventurous aspect of the charismatic leader, who, as de Man wrote in *Masses and Leaders*, is filled "with the great unquenchable desire to break free of bourgeois timidity, to live in a new, heroic era, governed by a more noble sort of authority than is conferred by property."[2]

Yet in contrast to the gambler or adventurer—or, for that matter, the career politician—the charismatic leader appears to his audience as an austere, trustworthy figure whose altruistic motives are beyond question. As French historian Alexander Dorna wrote:

> His speeches give the impression of truthfulness, honesty, and seriousness, which stand in marked contrast to the wooden language of run-of-the-mill politicians. . . . It's a feeling of authenticity that he communicates to his audience and that allows him to move them in direct, unmediated fashion. . . . The charismatic political speech is a collective High Mass via exclusively verbal means.[3]

Where de Man spoke of the leader's ability "to empathize his way into others' souls," the National Socialist theory of *"Führertum"* went a step further, distinguishing between charismatic leadership and mere dictatorship by declaring Hitler nothing less than "the personality of the community."[4] The idea was that the leader was a kind of vessel that contained and incarnated the soul of a people, articulating its will. In his 1936 study of National Socialist theories of law and legitimacy, French legal scholar Robert Bonnard explained:

Groundbreaking for the autobahn. Hitler, charismatic leader, at work for his people.

The leader's power rests on his personal authority. At the same time, it is also legitimated by the fact that he himself is intensely permeated by the spirit of the people,

> that the people exercise their power through him. . . .
> Thus the people are only obeying themselves when they
> follow the will of their leader.

In reality, Bonnard acknowledged, the notion of the people obeying their own will via the conduit of a charismatic dictator is pure myth. Yet insofar as the masses had faith in it, the belief exercised the same enormous psychosocial cohesive force as do all legends and religions. "National Socialism," Bonnard concluded, "owes its strength to this mythological foundation."[5]

Roosevelt's Radio and Hitler's Rally

While Hitler's and Roosevelt's nearly simultaneous ascension to power highlighted fundamental differences in politics, ideology, social background, and personality, contemporary observers also noted that they shared an extraordinary ability to touch the soul of the people. Their speeches were personal, almost intimate. Both in their own way gave their audiences the impression that they were addressing not the crowd, but each listener as an individual.

The explanation for Roosevelt's gift has to do with his preferred means of communication: the radio. Intimacy and directness were an intrinsic part of the medium. The listener sat as if face to face with a speaker who was no longer an orator, while the wireless gave the leader access to the most intimate social unit, the family, and allowed him to direct his message at each member personally. Thanks to radio, the distance between public speakers and their audiences, which had grown ever greater and more anonymous with the advent of mass democracy, suddenly and radically shrank. Radio may have lacked the force and magnetism generated by the physical presence of a mass audience. But this was more than compensated for by what Marshall McLuhan calls the illusion of "the electrical Eden, in which the Ego is absorbed into technology."

The wireless was the acoustic equivalent of film, the first great dream factory and media intoxicant that gave audiences the illusion of being at the center of things. Audiences perceived the solitude of the darkened cinema and the cozy spot in front of the radio not as isolation but as involvement. Radio enveloped the audience in what was being communicated more closely, intimately, hermetically, and totally than ever before. The disembodied voice on the radio was comparable to the visual images of silent movies in that both swept the audience into a kind of psychological undertow. Audience members couldn't help but use their imaginations to fill in the gaps that resulted from the absence of a sensual dimension—the sound in silent film and the visuals in radio. Receiving, in effect, only half the reality, the audience would supply the other half according to their own wishes, fantasies, and convictions. The panic that broke out in the greater New York area in 1938 after Orson Welles's broadcast of "The War of the Worlds" is but one example of the power of the mass imagination when it is called upon to supplement a scenario it has experienced only acoustically.

To quote a 1935 study on the subject: "Voices have a way . . . of arousing a train of imagination that will conjure up a substantial and congruent personality to support and harmonize with the disembodied voice."[6] Radio listeners credited Roosevelt with possessing "a golden voice" that was "fresh," "pleasant," "rich," "brilliant," and "melodious,"[7] and they transferred those attributes to Roosevelt as a person. As John G. Carlile from CBS put it at the time, "President Roosevelt's voice reveals sincerity, goodwill and kindness, determination, conviction, strength, courage and abounding happiness."[8] The sound of Roosevelt's voice was convincing, suggestive, and authoritative—regardless of what he was saying. One 1930s rhetoric researcher was led to conclude that "if Herbert Hoover had spoken the same words [as FDR's Inaugural Address] into the microphone . . . the stock market would have fallen another notch and public confidence with it."[9]

In dubbing his national radio addresses "fireside chats," Roosevelt created a brand name for this type of mass-media intimacy. Scant weeks after taking office, he was already being titled the "radio president" and had become the target for caricaturists and satirists. John Dos Passos referred to him sarcastically as the "you-and-me President."[10] Roosevelt's style of intonation was better suited to the radio than any of his predecessors' or rivals'. Their appearances on radio consisted of traditional-style political addresses that were broadcast via the medium without being tailored to it. Roosevelt's addresses were different. In June 1933, Orrin Dunlap, the media critic of the *New York Times*, wrote, "Whereas the others perorated, he chats." Roosevelt's rival Alf Landon was "a disaster" in this regard, wrote French observer Bernard Fay: "In spite of the diction lessons he received, supposedly from an English actor . . .

and in spite of his heroic efforts to adapt, when he was in front of a microphone, he looked like a fish in a fish bowl, staring out from behind the glass."[11]

Roosevelt's lack of a grand rhetorical style proved to be an advantage in the radio era, just as naturalistic actors benefited from the advent of film, leaving behind their stage colleagues who used anachronistic, large gestures.[12] At the same time, Roosevelt's success was not solely the product of innate talent. His radio addresses were carefully structured and systematically rehearsed. Just as Hitler tried out gestures in front of a mirror, Roosevelt practiced his fireside chats, experimenting with variations in articulation, intonation, tempo, length of pauses, and choice of words. One of his basic rules was to restrict himself wherever possible to the most commonly used words in American English. He also inserted a false tooth before every one of his radio addresses to eliminate a slight hiss in his voice that was scarcely noticeable in his real-life speech. Roosevelt consciously distinguished between radio and everyday speech, realizing that each followed its own specific dramatic rules. For that reason, he sometimes refused to allow his live speeches to be broadcast over the airwaves.

Contemporaries were quick to take note of Roosevelt's well-practiced ability to convince the ordinary listener that the president was addressing him directly and "that the Administration was thinking specifically of him, that he had a place in society."[13] Writing in the *New York Times*, Dunlap called Roosevelt's fireside chats "heart-to-heart talks with all America" and quoted one of the program directors for the NBC broadcasting network:

The "you-and-me president" conducts a fireside chat.

"The unusual gift of making listeners feel, even though they may be hundreds of miles away, that he is talking with then instead of at them, is the key to Mr. Roosevelt's success on the air. . . . The unseen audience feels as if the President were agreeing with them about something they always believed."

Dunlap attributed this gift to Roosevelt's ability to imagine millions of listeners when he was speaking into the microphone: "His voice carries a feeling of intimacy with his audiences as well as with his subject. He seems to be talking instead of reading. He apparently visualizes his millions of listeners, and through this feeling of close contact with them, makes them feel close to him."

Roosevelt's secretary of labor, Francis Perkins, reflecting on the recording of a fireside chat in the White House, observed: "His face would smile and light up as though he were actually sitting on the front porch or in the parlor with them." The audience's reaction was much the same. One of Roosevelt's aides reported back to the White House, "People down here all seem to think they know the President personally! . . . They feel he is talking to each of them." The aide also cited a satis-fied individual listener: "He makes us all feel that he is talking directly to us as individuals."[14]

THE INTIMATE LINK that Roosevelt forged via his fireside chats differed from the celebrations of unity between the people and their leader staged at major Nazi Party rallies. Yet both were collective experiences. As divergent as the media of the radio and the party rally were in many respects, the end result—a new kind of "electric" connection between the speaker and the mass audience—was much the same. Ernst Hanfstaengl, one of Hitler's earliest friends and allies, once noted:

> Those who know Hitler only from his appearances in later years—a demagogue and dictator boundlessly rant-ing and raving at the microphone—have no idea what a subtle and mellifluous instrument his nonamplified voice was at the time of his political debut. His baritone was both gentle and resonant. His gutturals gave listeners goose bumps. His vocal chords were still fresh and

allowed him to produce nuances that had a unique effect. . . . His rhetorical style was often reminiscent of the playing technique of a master violinist, who seldom runs the full length of the bow over the strings, so that the sound is less a fully fledged tone than the intimation of an idea.[15]

Our post-1945 impression of Hitler's speeches is deceptive. As a rule, what we know of his oratory consists of excerpts, aggressive, often hoarse passages in which his staccato-fortissimo dominates.

But these were only a part of his speeches, and often not the part that had the greatest effect on the audience. As rhetorician Ulrich Ulonska noted in 1990, Hitler's speeches typically followed the tripartite structure of classical oratory—or, musically speaking, Beethoven's *Pastoral*. Ulonska writes:

Hitler usually begins calmly with anecdotes and seemingly objective descriptions of facts. In particular, he invokes the values and desires of his audience, and in so doing portrays himself as one of them and appeals for their trust. . . . There are no wild affects in this phase of his speeches.

The second phase is dominated by defamations and insults. Hitler awakens untamed emotion . . . he creates an enormous amount of interpersonal tension by depicting the values and needs of his listeners as being under threat. He calls forth fear, worry, desperation, and the desire for salvation and a leader to show the way out of danger.

All of Hitler's speeches conclude with a positive, constructive phase. There are fewer and fewer defamations. Hitler releases his listeners from the tension that he previously induced by offering them a vision of a better

future attainable through the achievement of certain top-
ically specific goals. . . . With emotional force and conviction, Hitler simultaneously sets out the ethical basis
for the better days to come and positions himself as an
example of moral integrity. With that, he elevates himself
to a position of symbolic rescuer, moral savior, and collective superego for everyone in attendance.[16]

An internal party directive from 1937 confirms the importance of constructive, positive elements in the Nazi use of psychological suggestion. "A clever tactician," the author asserted,
"will move on to the negative, critical portion of his speech
after an appropriate introduction in which he has acquainted
the audiences with his subject matter and basic thoughts.
Never should more than half of the total speaking time be
devoted to negation."

Ulonska speculates that Rudolf Bartels's *Demagogues'
Primer*—like Gustave Le Bon's *Psychology of the Masses*, published in 1905—was a main inspiration for Hitler's rhetorical
style. Indeed, a passage from that work reads like the key to
understanding the effect achieved by Hitler's regular rhetorical
outbreaks of anger: "A strong moral sensibility expresses itself
in strong terms. . . . Words of exasperation and horror can be a
sign that the person using them has a strong sense of right and
wrong. . . . The connection between symptom and mood is
what makes frequent and strenuous utterance of moral disgust
so very valuable. They are one of the most effective means of
convincing the masses."[17]

Hitler exploited the techniques of classical rhetoric to establish a relationship of trust with his audience. But the staging of
his speeches, which incorporated theatrical, musical, military,

and religious elements, was anything but classical or traditional. Hitler biographer Joachim Fest has described them as "a hybrid between circus, grand opera, and Catholic liturgy."[18] Staging was crucial to Hitler's ability to convince his audience that there was a profound connection between the speaker and his listeners. Extrarhetorical elements were not just background accoutrements, as the decorations and musical programs of traditional political meetings had been. In the words of historian Detlef Grieswelle, they "merged with the speech to form an organic whole."[19] The darkened auditorium, the blaring military music, the marching formations of the SA under a sea of flags and standards, and the dramatic effects of spotlight illumination created a collective space in which Hitler, after keeping his audience waiting in a nearly excruciating state of expectation, could make his grand appearance as the messianic savior.[20]

It was a special kind of messiah who addressed the crowd at the beginning of these sermons. Hitler took the stage not as a Siegfriedesque superman but, rather, as one of the common people, the faceless foot soldier whose every speech reenacted his rise, election, and accession to the position of supreme leader. In 1936 Konrad Heiden remarked, "Hitler knew enough about the dramatics of lighting to remain only half-visible during his public appearances. Entering the hall, he would hurry through the ranks of the SA so that for most of the audience he remained a fleeting, blurry apparition."[21] Beginning modestly, as though unsure of whether he could find words for what he wanted to say, Hitler gave his audiences the illusion that one of them had raised his voice to articulate the common will. Countless eyewitness accounts from foreign observers attest to what Joachim Fest calls the "copulatory character"[22] of Hitler's mass rallies. "He played the crowd like a gigantic organ," noted one eyewitness, "pulling out all the stops, permitting the listeners to rave and roar, laugh and cry. But inevitably the stream flowed back, until a fiery alternating current welded speaker and listeners into one."[23] Another reported:

> Hitler responds to the vibrations of the human heart with the sensitivity of a seismograph . . . proclaiming the most secret desires, the least admissible instincts, the sufferings and personal revolts of a whole nation. His words go like an arrow to their target, he touches every private wound on the raw, liberates the mass unconscious, expressing its innermost aspirations, telling it what it most wants to hear.[24]

And a third observer commented, "Even at the biggest events, every individual listener has the feeling that the Führer is speaking directly to him. That's the source of the tremendous affection and loyalty poured out by every individual toward this man."[25]

What Hitler himself referred to as his ability to "mix" people—that is, to transform them into a mass with which he himself could then merge—Konrad Heiden called a capacity for "inner transpiration," by which he meant "the state of complete permeation by the feeling of being nothing more than a unit of a single, homogeneous community of will, faith, and, if necessary, action." At Hitler's rallies, Heiden asserted, "there were no passive listeners, just active participants."[26] "The masses," Heiden remarked on another occasion, "feel that this man is themselves, an aggregate and personification of their own forces."[27]*

Theodor W. Adorno later explained the tendency of the masses to identify with what he called the "great little man" in Freudian terms, as the simultaneous dissolution of the ego ideal in the figure of the leader-hero and the preservation of the ego's narcissism by means of identifying with the "little" aspect of the leader. As Adorno writes, "The superman must still resemble the follower and appear as his 'enlargement.' Accordingly, one of the devices of personalized fascist propaganda is the concept of the 'great little man,' a person who suggests both omnipotence and the idea that he is just one of the folks."[28]

FOR ALL THE similarities between Hitler's and Roosevelt's methods of "merging with the masses," it is important to note that they were coming from fundamentally different positions. Hitler was a true political outsider. In Germany, "liturgical" political demonstrations were *the* instrument for winning over the crowds in the struggle for power between 1920 and

---

*The case was somewhat different with Mussolini. According to historian Pierre Milza, Mussolini's mass rallies were less concerned with liturgical than with ludic or festive effects: "In a country in which the lyric arts are king and in which representations of the sacred are surrounded by flamboyant scenery, what many Italians liked about the fascist liturgy was its theatrical character . . . the long periods chanted in a powerful voice from the balcony of the Palazzo Venezia . . . the phases, the tirades delivered *mezzo voce*, the provocative gesture that looks funny to us today but needs to be resituated within its own context and its own time" (*Mussolini* [Paris, 1999], pp. 561–62).

1932—they set the whole process of charismatic crystallization in motion. After 1933, Hitler restricted his appearances to formal celebrations such as the annual Party rallies in Nuremberg. Having attained total power, he no longer needed to win over the crowd—indeed, that would have been an insult to his authority. Whereas he had previously had to conquer the masses—to "incarnate" them, so to speak—in order to attain the status of absolute leader, his post-1933 appearances aimed at reinforcing his iconic status, making it impervious to the vagaries of public opinion. Maintaining that image was a main task of propaganda about Hitler.[29]

The primary difference between Hitler's and Roosevelt's situations was, of course, that Roosevelt, even after taking office, was never without political opposition. He may not have gone through a period of political struggle comparable to Hitler's between 1920 and 1932, but neither did he enjoy absolute, unquestioned political authority. Even as a sitting president, he remained a constant campaigner.

Roosevelt's fondness for radio can thus also be explained by the necessity of having to reinforce his hard-won charisma in daily competition with an autonomous opposition. Significantly, Roosevelt only began using the radio after he was elected. (He first discovered the medium while serving as governor of New York.) Radio, as a means of technological reproduction, was the ideal format for continually replicating Roosevelt's public persona. Moreover, according to the American consensus of the time, radio was not only the most effective but also the most rational of the mass media. Since the late nineteenth century, mass live events had been considered dangerous because crowds were subject to their own uncanny, ungovernable dynamic. In contrast, 1930s social psychologists saw the community of radio listeners as a collection of individuals who would never lose their heads because they were not physically brought together in a single homogeneous mass. "We do not feel the compulsion to conform or to express the feelings that others are expressing," wrote the authors of a 1935 volume entitled *The Psychology of the Radio*. "We are less emotional and more critical, less crowdish and more individualistic."[30] Some sociologists even credited the advanced state of radio culture in the United States with preserving liberal democracy. As a corrective to rallies, which left the crowd open to demagogic, totalitarian brainwashing, radio was deemed the best guarantee for "a detoxified crowd that could be bent to the purposes of enlightened leaders."[31]

Such paeans to the innately beneficial, democratic quality of radio appear less than convincing in light of the high regard the medium enjoyed in Europe's concurrent dictatorships. Yet in Italy and Germany, the popularity of radio began only with the rise of the totalitarian systems; when Hitler and Mussolini took power, neither of their nations had a mass radio culture. By contrast, when Roosevelt assumed office, radio was already popular in America. In 1932, Americans owned 16 million of some 20 million existing wireless receivers in the world. Even in the most technologically advanced nations of Europe radio was still in its infancy, its programming and the listening habits of its audience at an experimental stage. While the claims for radio's democraticizing effect are hard to substantiate, there is no question that radio culture was essential for the American way of projecting political charisma.

Thus, the success of Roosevelt's fireside chats cannot be attributed solely to his harmonious, trust-inspiring voice or to his ability to empathize with the listeners and touch their souls. Just as the effects of Hitler's choreographed ceremonies can be understood only with reference to the psychological and cultural disposition of his audience, Roosevelt's radio triumphs were possible only because the new medium had programmed his audience in a specific psychological and cultural way. Without insisting on a direct causal connection, cultural theorist Warren Susman points to the genre of the soap opera as a critical influence. Well established by the time of Roosevelt's fireside chats, the soap opera had brought with it a set of audience expectations and behavioral responses that may well have prepared listeners to respond personally when Roosevelt entered their living rooms.[32]

The soap opera evolved as a result of advertisers discovering housewives as their target audience. Previously, radio programming had concentrated on the evening, the time of day in which the family would congregate around the wireless. The programs offered were often plays or musical performances that, just as in a cinema, concert hall, or theater, required the audience's full concentration. The soap opera changed all that, and thereby people's listening habits. Soap operas did not require concentration. They were aural wallpaper, forever present in the background, while the housewife went about her daily chores. In the process, the radio went from being a device that transmitted discrete performances to one that kept the listener company and provided a kind of sonic ether in which she moved about. It was part of life and part of the listener's soul, as well as a sign of

The opposite of mass-media domestic intimacy: Hitler Youth at radio attention

material well-being. A study carried out by the Rockefeller Foundation in 1939 concluded that for unemployed families radio had become an important source of moral and psychological support, the loss of which would have been considered a sign of absolute impoverishment.[33]

BOTH THE WAY in which people listened to the soaps and the stories themselves—ordinary and familiar—served to blur the distinctions between fiction and reality, fantasy and daily life. Unlike such traditional escapist media as literature and film, which were enjoyed for a specific and limited period of time, the soaps were ongoing. And in contrast to traditional escapist culture, the soap heroines were not the brides, daughters, or heiresses of millionaires but came from the same social background as their audiences. They were replacement neighbors, replacement friends, and replacement selves whose presence on the radio was like a "daily visit" from an idealized alter ego. According to critic Eckhard Breitinger, the soap opera was for its listeners "a fairy tale come true, a substitute reality that carefully conceals its function as substitute." Breitinger cites an early example of product placement whereby listeners could order a brooch supposedly worn by the heroine from the soap opera's sponsor. The fetishistic character of such souvenirs is familiar, but the attraction involved was different from the traditional cult around media stars in that it was directed at a fictional character and not the actress who played her. Significantly, the fictional heroines of soap operas often received thousands of pieces of fan mail—sometimes even gifts from the audience.[34]

On the surface, there would seem to be an enormous difference between a participant at a mass Nazi rally and a radio soap-opera fan. The rally was a singular event of quasi-mythic and religious ecstasy, leading to the "inner transpiration" of the masses that identified with their leader; the soap opera, an utterly banal bit of routine aimed at housewives listening to the wireless while going about their daily chores. Yet in both cases, the end result was similar. The individual abandoned him- or herself fully to the speaker in return for the wish fulfillment of a fantasy audio world, which made listeners feel significant. A study on the psychology of soap-opera listeners from the late 1930s concluded that the soap opera

> directs the private reveries and fantasies of the listeners
> into socially approved channels of action and increases
> the woman's feeling of importance by showing that the
> family is of the highest importance and that she has con-
> trol over vicissitudes of family life. It thereby decreases
> their feeling of futility and makes them feel essential and
> wanted.[35]

In the end, the difference between Roosevelt's preference for radio dramatics and Hitler's and Mussolini's reliance on staged live events seems primarily the result of a technological and therefore cultural time lag. Whereas in Europe large physical congregations were still required to suggest and maintain the idea of political charisma, in the United States, with its more advanced mass media, the same psychological mechanisms were already obeying different rules. Even after the Fascists and the Nazis had saturated their respective nations with radio receivers, both regimes continued to place great emphasis on mass live events. As a matter of principle, Hitler and Mussolini never delivered their addresses from radio studios. In Hitler's case, this fact has usually been explained with reference to his sup-posed inability to communicate effectively in the absence of actual listeners.[36] But that is only one side of the story. Perhaps Hitler's refusal to do studio broadcasts also reflects his audi-ence's limited experience of radio culture and hence their inabil-ity to be enthralled by an oration not delivered in person. That his speeches at rallies became even more important after the introduction of the *"Volksempfänger"* (people's radio) argues for a kind of inertia, a reluctance to forgo the familiarity of mass gatherings. This also explains the Nazis' otherwise senseless insistence on broadcasting those speeches via strategically posi-

"All Germany listens to the Führer on the People's Radio." Even after most families had radios in their homes, Germans were reluctant to forgo the familiarity of mass gatherings.

tioned loudspeakers in urban areas, regardless of the fact that most German families had a wireless receiver in their homes. Apparently, it was felt that individuals or small groups gathered around the radio would be less susceptible to Hitler's sway than would crowds pressed together around public loudspeakers on city streets and squares.[37]

The Americanization of Europe after 1945 shows how backward the Continent was in terms of mass-media culture and psychology in the 1930s. Today, the only occasions when masses of people come together and experience something like "inner transpiration" are sporting events and rock concerts. Political charisma nowadays is projected exclusively in the television studio.

· 3 ·

PROPAGANDA

The most damning blow that the dictatorships have struck at democracy has been the compliment they have paid us in taking over (and perfecting) our most prized devices of persuasion and our underlying contempt for the credulity of the masses.

Max Lerner, 1934[1]

Propaganda is the means by which charismatic leadership, circumventing intermediary social and political institutions like parliaments, parties, and interest groups, gains direct hold upon the masses. It is to the will of a regime what the automatic transmission is to an automobile engine. Explicit state propaganda rarely exists in liberal-democratic societies because their constitutions prohibit the executive from controlling public opinion—just as governments are prohibited from directing the economy. Only in periods of crisis may the legislative branch of government grant the executive the right to intervene in either area.

This happened for the first time on a broad international front during World War I, and nowhere among the combatants, in comparison with the prewar situation, did state intervention proceed more radically than in the United States. In the aftermath of that conflict, propaganda fell into moral disrepute, as public opinion came to see the state's wartime control over the media as a noxious, indeed un-American over-reaction. The rise of totalitarianism in Europe between the two world wars only strengthened this antipathy, as propaganda was viewed and practiced by those regimes not as a necessary evil but as a legitimate means of articulating national interests. Of course, political systems at the time were careful to term their own attempts to steer public opinion "education" and "infor-mation," while accusing their rivals of practicing propaganda. Only National Socialism—which created a special government department for "Public Enlightenment and Propaganda"—freely admitted there was no real difference between the two.

Harold D. Lasswell, the author of a seminal 1930s study on enforced conformity in public opinion during World War I, agreed that the line between education and propaganda was essentially a matter of perspective. Characterizing American understanding of the two concepts, he concluded, "The spread of controversial attitudes is propaganda; the spread of accepted attitudes is skills education. It is proper to speak of Commu-nism as propaganda in Chicago and as education in Moscow."[2]

It's easy to recognize parallels in the perceived contrast between irrational, dangerous propaganda and rational, con-structive programs of educational information, and the distinc-tion, common in 1930s American radio theory, between the irrational "crowd" and the rational public. The conclusion of American theorists that radio was an innately rational medium for the dissemination of information, went hand in hand with the belief that the collective social will expressed in government information programs in a democracy was above any kind of dictatorial propaganda and aimed merely at educating the public.

Regardless of whether they spoke of propaganda or of education, National Socialists and New Dealers agreed that neither conceived of the process as funneling information from above down to the masses. On the contrary, the first step in educating and influencing the masses was always to find out what those masses themselves thought and desired. Joseph Goebbels has been quoted as saying,

> The government must diagnose with almost scientific precision the people's soul and must be informed of all psychological trends in the citizenry. It must illuminate the people if these trends lead nowhere, or it must recognize the opinions of the people if their opinions are justified.[3]

In the Third Reich, the collection and evaluation of information about public opinion was carried out by the thirty-two regional branches of the Ministry of Propaganda, the various local party chapters, the Security Service, and the Gestapo. The corresponding institutions in New Deal America were the local chapters of the Democratic Party and the National Emergency Council, which was founded in 1933, as well as various governmental agencies and the White House itself. Moreover, as the focus of the Roosevelt administration shifted in the late 1930s from domestic reforms to American intervention in international affairs, the need to influence rather than just to research popular opinion increased, leading to the formation of further public relations departments, such as the Office of Facts and Figures in 1940.[4]

Letters to the president provided one main source of information. In his fireside chats, Roosevelt explicitly called upon listeners to put their feelings down in writing, and he often read such letters during his addresses as evidence that his government's programs were responding to the public's wishes. Collecting information about and influencing public opinion thus formed a closed plebiscitary circle.[5] Its success is evident in the fact that Roosevelt received ten times as much mail at the White House than had his predecessor, Herbert Hoover.

The government institutions in Washington and Berlin responsible for collecting and disseminating information grew in size and number at roughly the same rate after 1933. Thus, both qualitatively and quantitatively, the public relations work undertaken by the Roosevelt administration and the Hitler regime was unlike anything that had come before. John A. Garraty, the pioneer of historical comparisons between National Socialism and the New Deal, called the American campaigns "unparalleled among democracies," adding, "Roosevelt did not create a propaganda machine even remotely comparable to Goebbels', but under the New Deal the government undertook efforts unprecedented in peacetime."[6] To staff its recently formed departments and institutions, the new administration unabashedly raided the Washington press corps. Elisha Hanson, a leading representative of the Association of American Publishers at the time, noted sarcastically that "more newspapermen write news for the Government than are employed by the newspapers and press associations to write for them."[7]

Organizationally, the main difference between Washington and Berlin was that Nazi propaganda was steered by a single central ministry, whereas the New Deal split that responsibility between various agencies. Government departments that had previously had a press office consisting of a spokesman, a secretary, and perhaps an assistant suddenly created whole sub-departments for press and public relations work. Seventy-three press liaisons worked in the Department of Agriculture, twenty-three in the Federal Housing Administration, and twenty-one on the Social Security Board.[8] Their job was to flood the nation with positive information about governmental policies and projects. As a commentator remarked at the time, such governmental "handouts" represented "the backbone of most of the news stories which you read today in your daily newspaper under Washington date-lines."[9]

The American press remained free. Unlike their German colleagues, who were subject to control and censorship, American journalists took no direct orders from the government. Ignoring government information did not entail any sanctions, and the press, which turned increasingly anti-Roosevelt after 1934, often did precisely that. Yet we should beware of simplified contrasts between the free and the nonfree press. Recent historical research has suggested that Nazi control of the press "in actual practice was less totalitarian than National Socialism itself wanted to depict and many historians still think it was."[10] Once the initial period of co-option and disciplinary measures was over, those journalists who still had jobs accepted National Socialism as an unavoidable reality. Mere knowledge of the consequences of noncompliance with the often unwritten rules sufficed to encourage most of them to toe the line, and enforce the most effective and invisible form of control—self-censorship. Totalitarian propaganda, in any case, wasted no opportunity to heap scorn upon the liberal claim to complete freedom of speech. To Fascist sensibilities, the idea itself was nothing but propaganda.

IN CONTRAST TO the traditional hagiography of Roosevelt as a democratic leader, some recent researchers have argued that the New Deal took care to keep the press under its thumb. Historian David Culbert, for example, writes:

> From today's perspective, one can almost admire the skill with which the democratic leadership under the president persuaded the public it was maintaining complete freedom of speech and the press in order to . . . limit those freedoms. The *cooptation* of the press, i.e., the invitation to cooperate voluntarily, proved to be enormously effective.[11]

This view overstates the case. Significant pressure to cooperate was brought to bear on newspapers only in the first year of the New Deal, when Roosevelt was riding the crest of an initial wave of popular enthusiasm. Once that receded, the print media, which were largely controlled by Republicans, turned against the New Deal. Moreover, the Roosevelt administration never sought in any direct form to curtail the right of freedom of the press.

But the situation was somewhat different with radio. Most contemporaries agreed that radio—like television today—had far more influence on the masses than the printed word, and radio, although it was organized commercially, was by no means completely in the hands of private owners. From the medium's very inception, the state functioned as the controlling authority—as the sovereign master of the airwaves, which, in the form of restricted broadcasting licenses, temporarily granted private entrepreneurs the use of *its* property. The Radio Act of 1927 required American broadcasters to serve "public interest, convenience or necessity." Broadcasting licenses were granted for three years, at which point they were up for review. If a broadcaster was found to have violated official requirements, he could lose his right to use the airwaves. Because most stations focused on the utterly conformist genre of the soap opera, the threat of license revocation remained hypothetical. In the largely apolitical, mass-consumer-oriented society of the 1920s, no conflicts between public and private interest in radio arose.

The U.S. Communications Act of 1934, however, restricted the duration of broadcasting licenses to six months. Simultaneously, Roosevelt appointed one of his most faithful party stalwarts as chairman of the Federal Communications Commission. Shortly thereafter, radio stations were required to submit transcripts of all programs "on public affairs" for FCC approval, and an FCC member let it be known that airing programs critical of the government could lead to broadcasting licenses being revoked.[12] Thus it was not without some justification that a 1935 German Ph.D. dissertation on American broadcasting laws concluded, "State control is a reality in America today."[13]

In fact, the situation was less one of total control or censorship than of a desire among broadcasters, especially the three major radio networks, to maintain cordial relations with the government. Just as it was always mindful not to alienate advertisers, the radio industry often tried to anticipate and conform to the desires of the government. Hugh Johnson, an early member of the Roosevelt administration, was promptly fired from his job as a radio commentator when he turned against FDR. His dismissal came not in response to a request by the White House but at the personal initiative of NBC head Frank Russell.[14] Furthermore, in 1934, when the FCC called upon NBC to allot more airtime to the government for educational programming, the station could point out that it had already devoted more than 250 hours to such content. Radio stations did not need to be told what to say. Usually they were already saying it.

The Power of Symbols

In a conversation with Hermann Rauschning, the National Socialist who later broke with the party and fled Germany in 1936, Adolf Hitler revealed the origins of his preferred method for influencing public opinion. "I've learned a lot from Marxism," Hitler said, adding:

> Fundamentally, these new means of political struggle can be traced back to the Marxists. I only needed to adopt and further develop them, and I essentially had what we needed. I just had to continue, with greater resolve, where the Social Democrats had failed ten times over because they insisted on trying to achieve their revolution within the framework of democracy. National

> Socialism is what Marxism could have been if it had
> freed itself from its absurd, artificial connection with the
> democratic system.[15]

Hitler was also greatly taken with socialists' use of heraldic red as the symbolic color of the party. He recalled his impressions from a mass Communist rally in Berlin: "There was a sea of red flags, red armbands, and red flowers at the event . . . even superficially, it was an impressive sight. I myself could feel and understand how easily the man on the street could fall under the suggestive spell of such a grandiose spectacle."[16]

Among the other sources National Socialism drew upon were the rites and symbols of the Catholic Church, the formations and decor of the military, and the techniques of modern, American-style advertising. In its capacity for universal appropriation, the Nazi Party was anything but historically unique. Symbols continuously consume and are consumed by other symbols, forming a constant accompaniment to the changes of real power they come to represent—be it the adoption of pagan rituals and symbols by Christianity, the appropriation of Christian liturgy by secular revolutions, or the use of all of the above, and indeed every available historical source, in advertising.

In the 1930s the symbol came to be considered the main unit of currency in political propaganda, an effective "short-cut to understanding and action," in the words of early propaganda expert Edward Bernays. For Harold Lasswell, propaganda amounted to "the manipulation of collective attitudes by the use of significant symbols (words, pictures, tunes) rather than violence, bribery or boycott." Yet if propaganda could do the work of violence, Lasswell concluded, the inverse was equally valid; violence could be an act of propaganda: "An act of violence becomes 'propaganda of the deed' when it is expected that the effect on attitudes will be highly disproportionate to the immediate objective consequences of the act."[17] That statement holds true in equal measure for both revolutionary and state-instituted terrorism.

Before we proceed to consider the creation and use of symbols by the New Deal and the Third Reich, we might as a kind of prelude look at an episode from the final years of the Weimar Republic. Occupying a minor place in the annals of propaganda, the "war of symbols," as it was known, deserves closer inspection.[18]

In September 1930, the National Socialists scored a victory in national elections that made them the strongest party in the Reichstag. The Nazis' electoral success was a chilling wake-up call for Germany's social-democratic center, showing that the means by which the Fascists had conquered the streets could also be used to storm the country's political institutions and the state itself. The lesson was doubly bitter. On the one hand, democratic centrists were forced to recognize that the masses apparently welcomed methods that they themselves had rejected as demagogic, pseudorevolutionary, and quasi-religious, while their own rational arguments met with general indifference or, worse, inspired it. On the other hand, they realized to their horror that the methods the Nazis had used so successfully were nothing more than mimicry of the culture of political militancy that the social-democratic movement itself had pioneered in the nineteenth century.

Dumbstruck by the Nazis' success, the leaders of the political center responded by insisting even more stringently on rational argumentation and political pedagogy. Yet within the Social Democratic Party (SPD), a minority of young members drew the opposite conclusion, arguing that National Socialism had to be fought with its own means. They urged their comrades to stop trying to counter, or, as Julius Leber sarcastically put it, to "refute" the emotions, fantasies, fears, and actual suffering of the masses with rational argumentation. The rebels called their movement the Iron Front.

The specifics of their new strategy were, however, not a homegrown product but were based on the insights of a young Russian immigrant.

SERGEI CHAKOTIN CAME to propaganda via biology and zoology. A student and colleague of renowned behavioral psychologist Ivan Pavlov, Chakotin was the first to apply the theory of Pavlovian reflexes to the idea of mass suggestion. Having been politicized by the February and October revolutions of 1917, he put his insights in the service of anti-Bolshevism. After relocating to Germany and in the face of the increasingly likely National Socialist revolution, he felt called to protect his adopted homeland from succumbing to dictatorship. Chakotin drew his inspiration from three sources: the past achievements of the social democrats, his own personal experiences during the October Revolution, and the model of National Socialist propaganda. Chakotin urged the SPD to concentrate on emotional appeals to the electorate, avoiding the emotional vacuum and "pathetic doctrinaire tedium" of traditional social-democratic agitation.[19] Instead of boring gatherings, he argued, the party should stage dynamic events. Instead of endless debates and discussions, the party should devote itself to grand gestures and bold demonstrations—not of victimization but of power, purpose, and determination. As though taking a page from the propaganda section in *Mein Kampf*, Chakotin proposed that social democrats limit their agitation to a handful of the most popular slogans and symbols. These were to be repeated—indeed, hammered in—until they became part of the collective subconscious.

Chakotin's most significant contribution was the emblem used by the Iron Front. Inspired in equal measure by Russian Constructivism and the Nazi swastika, the logo featured a red background sliced through by three powerful arrows (either black or white), moving diagonally down from the top right as though attacking prey on the bottom left. That was precisely the intended association. The emblem conveyed the idea that the swastika was no longer just the attacker but itself under attack. Tested out during several 1932 regional elections, Chakotin's concept proved its mass appeal, helping the social democrats lure away Nazi voters. But the mainstream leadership rejected suggestions that the party adopt the image on the national level. Fearful of anything that might inflame the masses beyond the party's control, the leadership acted much as it had during the Revolution of 1918, persisting in its rational, moderate course until that, too, was destroyed by the triumphant Nazis.

The Iron Front episode yields different, more sober insights into the imitation and adoption of propagandistic symbols than the Nazis' successful cooption of socialist images. For even if the SPD leadership had embraced Chakotin's concept, it is unlikely that the end of the Weimar Republic could have been averted.

Chakotin's emblem for the Iron Front calls on Social Democrats to crush pro-Hitler industrialists.

Propagandistic symbols alone cannot resuscitate an essentially passive and moribund political body. It is one thing when an aggressive, unscrupulous, but also dynamic and innovative party like the National Socialists raids the symbolic arsenal of its enemies. It is another when the sheep tries to don the wolf's clothing. Propaganda without real power is nothing but bluster. Propaganda works best in the service of a movement that is already on the rise, and its most effective moment comes in periods of crisis and revolution, when a fading regime is losing its potency and the nation's will is as yet undecided. Then propaganda can tip the scales, and its slogans articulate the as-yet nebulous popular will. This tipping of the scales is probably what Harold Lasswell had in mind when he defined propaganda as a substitute for coercion and violence.

Let us see now how the New Deal coordinated symbolism and coercion in its major propaganda campaigns.

The Blue Eagle

The Blue Eagle campaign was an initiative undertaken by the National Recovery Administration to bring the free-falling economy under control. Its centerpiece was a symbol to be displayed by producers and retailers who complied with NRA standards, and the public, in turn, was encouraged to buy only from those outlets out of a sense of patriotic duty. The campaign began in July 1933, after Roosevelt's first hundred days in office—that is, at the point when popular enthusiasm for a new broom in the White House had run its course and the nation was threatening to relapse into the passive and despondent mood of the first three years of the Great Depression.

The Blue Eagle initiative was a good illustration of the old sports adage that the best defense is a good offense. The central reforms of the Roosevelt administration's inaugural period—the much-touted new state regulations on industrial production—had yielded few concrete results. The cotton industry was alone among America's large business sectors in accepting the rules with which the government hoped to end the economic crisis. Elsewhere, the NRA's codes concerning self-imposed price and wage controls, restrictions on production, child labor, and union involvement remained stuck in desk drawers or buried in piles of papers.

Whereas Roosevelt had easily succeeded in getting Congress to grant his executive branch broad emergency powers, he was in danger of failing utterly in his efforts to bring American industry under control. The way forward was obvious. Just as he had used the threat of public disapproval to bring Congress into line, so he now brought to bear the pressure of public opinion to force industrialists to conform to the administration's wishes.

It was a two-pronged attack. Every employer in the United States—from the owner of a corner drugstore to Henry Ford—received a document entitled "President's Re-Employment Agreement," which asked the recipient to *personally* promise Roosevelt his support for certain guidelines, including a minimum wage of twelve to fifteen dollars a week and a prohibition on child labor. At the same time, Roosevelt took to the airwaves in a fireside chat and appealed to every citizen to back the program. Reviving the war analogy from his inaugural address, he characterized the campaign as a "great summer offensive against unemployment," and he argued for the necessity of distinguishing friend from foe:

> In war, in the gloom of night attack, soldiers wear a bright badge on their shoulders to be sure that comrades do not fire on comrades. On that principle, those who cooperate in this program must know each other at a glance. That is why we have provided a badge of honor for this purpose, a simple design with a legend, "We do our part," and I ask that all those who join with me shall display that badge prominently.[20]

The "badge" in question took the form of pins, posters, and statuettes that featured a blue eagle clutching a bundle of lightning bolts against a white backdrop. It was framed by the NRA logo and the words "We do our part." By wearing the emblem on his or her lapel or blouse, consumers could demonstrate their personal support for the president's policies.

A corresponding poster, hung in shopwindows or on factory gates, made it publicly known that a business had accepted NRA guidelines and was working to ensure that they were enforced. Conversely, the absence of a Blue Eagle emblem suggested that a person or business did not support Roosevelt and did not belong to the national army fighting the Depression, and that therefore that person or business was to be treated as an enemy. NRA head Hugh Johnson left no doubt as to the symbol's polarizing intention, proclaiming, "Those who are not with us are against us."[21]

The Blue Eagle campaign followed and intensified the bellicose line that had been part of Roosevelt's earliest New Deal rhetoric and strategy. It made explicit reference to the United States' wartime mobilization of 1917–18 and the measures that accompanied it: state control and direction of both the economy and the press; criminalization and prosecution of war critics; and the Creel Committee's restrictions on free speech—in short, the entire battery of compulsory and voluntary means with which American society had been brought into line with the government's wartime efforts. A number of experts from that period were enlisted to run the Blue Eagle campaign. Bernard Baruch, the finance magnate who had organized state control of American industry's wartime production, put forward his former assistant Hugh Johnson to run the NRA.

New York post office workers cheer the unfurling of the National Revovery Administration banner.

Johnson, in turn, hired two of the main organizers of the 1917 Liberty Bonds campaign—which had encouraged private citizens to invest in America's war effort in World War I— to work out the details for the Blue Eagle initiative. One of the few big names that were missing was George Creel himself,

the man Woodrow Wilson had put in charge of domestic propaganda to whip up enthusiasm for American intervention.
This was probably due to the controversial reputation Creel
had acquired as a ruthless supressor of dissent. Still, he likely
played a behind-the-scenes, advisory role in the Blue Eagle
initiative.

The Blue Eagle campaign—or, as Johnson called it, "the
greatest peace-time assault on a national enemy this country has
ever seen"[22]—lasted from July 24 to September 13, 1933. The
limited run of the project aimed at preventing it from becoming
hackneyed or shopworn in the public eye. The campaign had
begun with a gripping fireside chat, and it ended with a nineteen-
hour-long, celebratory parade down New York's Fifth Avenue in
which a quarter of a million people took part. Public interest and
excitement grew exponentially as the project drew to a close.
The idea was to create a bandwagon effect, a dynamic of group
psychology that, once launched by mass propaganda, would be
driven by its own momentum. Persuasion and coercion worked
hand in hand. As in the Liberty Bonds campaign, the project's
organization was both centralized and decentralized. From the
NRA's office in Washington, Johnson called upon the chambers
of commerce in all cities with more than ten thousand inhabitants not only to get their members to sign on to the codes but
to take over the local management of the campaign. The NRA's
central propaganda machine worked day and night to provide
the necessary incentives, reviving the so-called four-minute men
from World War I: hundreds of thousands of volunteers who
delivered prepared speeches on street corners, in cinemas, theaters, and churches.[23]

Those who signed on to the "President's Re-Employment Agreement" received a Blue Eagle poster for prominent display in their businesses. Their names and the names of their businesses were also printed on an "Honorable Mention" list hung on the wall of the nearest post office. But what happened to those who refused to get on board?

Johnson was anything but a model democrat. An authoritarian hothead who raged that Blue Eagle detractors deserved "a sock right on the nose," he considered the corporatism of the Italian Fascists a model worthy of emulation and saw his task as so important that, as he said, "this law stuff doesn't matter."[24] But even had he wanted to trample on the individual freedoms protected by the Constitution, as the comparatively powerless Falstaff to the New Deal's real power holders, Roosevelt and Baruch, he would probably not have been given the opportunity to do so.

Unlike the campaigns to mobilize the public for World War I, which had been a mixture of propaganda and real repression, the Blue Eagle project was careful to limit its activities to education and persuasion. The main addressee of the initiative was always the public at large, not specific individuals, and its main mode of encouraging potential detractors to cooperate was the threat of being seen as a public enemy. To quote Bernard Baruch:

> The best method of enforcement lies in the power of public opinion. If it is completely understood that those who are cooperating are soldiers against the common enemy within, and those who omit to act are on the other side, there will be little hanging back.[25]

Johnson put the matter more bluntly, when he said the task of the Blue Eagle campaign was "to put the enforcement of this law into the hands of the whole people."

But what if individual entrepreneurs, despite all this, still refused to sign on? For Johnson the solution was simple. He spoke of receiving thousands of complaints of non-compliance and the government's plan to explain the citizens' obligations to each and every detractor. The next step, he suggested, was to unleash the force of public opinion.[26]

What this meant in plain English was the threat of a boy-cott. Roosevelt had already made it clear that refusal to endorse NRA codes would mean that businesses would be denied gov-ernment contracts. Yet the government using the leverage of state contracts was one thing; it was another for Washington to call for public boycotts. Even Johnson realized that such a call was unconstitutional. Thus, he was careful to argue in a 1933 speech that "of course what people are doing is not a boycott." "The public," he added, "simply cannot tolerate non-compliance with their plan."[27]

In a fine example of doublespeak, the argument maintained that cooperation with the president was completely voluntary but that exceptions would not be tolerated because the will of the public was so unanimously behind FDR. As one historian put it, the Blue Eagle campaign was "based on voluntary coop-eration, but those who did not volunteer to cooperate were to be forced into participation."[28]

Commentators who were not New Deal adherents or part of the propaganda apparatus were under no illusion about the sleight of hand in this argument.[29] The Republican-owned *New York Herald Tribune* was the most shrill in its reaction, responding to the Blue Eagle program with prophesies of "a coercive force of the first magnitude and one likely to be no more reasonable than a lynching party."[30] William E. Berchtold was somewhat more moderate in a 1934 article for the *North American Review:* "The patriotic appeal of the Blue Eagle boycott blanketed the press more efficiently than any revealed censorship could have accomplished."[31] And in a 1935 book comparing Bolshevism, Fascism, National Socialism, and the New Deal, Ethan Colton concluded, "The bombardment of the public mind bore resemblance to the smashing propaganda drives put on by the Bolshevik and Nazi machines."[32]

British observers mocked the campaign as intolerant, humorless, and neurotically conformist. The *Economist* found the Blue Eagle initiative "strangely reminiscent of Whitehall in wartime," producing an atmosphere in which "criticism even of [the eagle's] heraldic merits is not too kindly taken." The *Spectator* echoed those sentiments: "War time psychology prevails. Criticism of the Government's efforts by American citizens is akin to treason, by foreigners to impertinence . . . and intolerance is accompanied by a signal lack of humour."[33] And reporting on the parade in New York, the *Daily Herald*'s correspondent wrote, "There were more Blue Eagles than Swastikas in Germany."[34]

French commentators agreed that the campaign's significance was more psychological than economic. Robert de Saint-Jean, for instance, described the project as "an extremely picturesque bit of theater" and a "wonderful revue." "The scenery constantly changes," Saint-Jean wrote, "as though the whole spectacle were being run by a director who is a master of his craft and knows that a scene—no matter how stirring—should never last for more than a minute."[35]

Simone-Maxe Benoit concluded that "the Blue Eagle campaign raised the people's morale over the course of the year, although its actual effect was less than expected."[36] The Marquis de La Londe concurred:

> The president cannot always fulfill the masses' perennial demands for both bread and circuses. But while his voters may not have sufficient bread, they're entertained all the more with circuses. The extravagant parades that they are offered, and let themselves by impressed by, compensate for what they lack.[37]

For Louis Rosenstock-Franck, the style of the Blue Eagle campaign *was* the substance of the New Deal. "Basically," he wrote, "it is a phenomenon consisting of movement and activism. [The New Deal] welds the nation together. But its worth is derived less from what it positively achieves than from its sheer existence and presence."[38] And Bernard Fay was convinced that Roosevelt's "care in his choice of means and his dramatic sense of how they're used" came together in "an overwhelming display of power" that no one in America could resist.[39]

Curiously, the German media, which otherwise followed the New Deal with such great interest, merely reported on the Blue Eagle campaign without offering any sort of substantive commentary.

"Symbolism of Compliance"

The phrase "symbolism of compliance" was coined by Fritz Morstein Marx, a high-ranking bureaucrat in the administration of the German city-state of Hamburg before 1933 and later a professor of administrative law at Harvard University. He applied it to expressions of loyalty by Germans toward the National Socialist regime. As examples, he cited the use of "Heil Hitler" as a form of greeting, the prominent display of swastika flags hanging from the windows of private homes, and the out-pouring of contributions to the Nazi Winter Relief charity.[40] These expressions of fealty were not officially required. In reality, of course, a kind of indirect compulsion did exist. Those who attracted attention to themselves through nonparticipation risked, in the best-case scenario, being subjected to scrutiny by the party's many official and unofficial spies. More often than not, they incurred harsher sanctions.

In 1933, Americans who did not publicly support the Blue Eagle campaign invited the threat of social ostracism or economic boycott—the results of which were no less devastating for having been brought about by the state's tacit recommendation, instead of by official decree. Germans who in the autumn of that same year did not hang swastikas from their windows, greet their fellow citizens with "Heil Hitler," or wear an emblem on their lapels identifying them as Winter Relief contributors could expect to receive significantly more severe forms of punishment. Nonetheless, it is impossible to ignore the similarity in approach for encouraging conformity. A closer look at the Winter Relief project provides a good example of the affinity.

Like the construction of the German autobahn and other prestige programs, the Winter Relief campaign was promoted as the realization on a grand scale of timid efforts begun during the Weimar Republic. It was initiated in the fall of 1933, six months after a general boycott on April 1, 1933, of Jewish-owned businesses had proved to be a minor public relations disaster. Called by the party leadership, not the government, the centrally organized boycott had seemed to be the best means of channeling and controlling rowdyism, which in the preceding weeks had threatened to get out of bounds. On the one hand it was to provide an outlet for the aggression of the revolutionary Nazi rank and file; on the other it would offer the party leadership a chance to demonstrate its competence. By simultaneously taking the lead in a "popular movement" and blunting that movement's potential for anarchic violence, the party's leaders could show both adherents and detractors that they were in control. But the action was only a partial success. While the boycott did succeed in stemming "untamed" attacks on Jewish-owned property, it failed to have the desired effects on either foreign or domestic popular opinion. On the contrary, the boycott highlighted the fact that discrimination against and persecution of Jews was official government policy. Admonitions by the Nazi leadership that participants were to carry out the boycott nonviolently did little to counteract images of Brownshirts posted in front of Jewish-owned businesses or the view of them as symbols of Nazi arbitrariness and repression of a defenseless minority. The boycott also failed to embody Germans' feelings of ethnic solidarity, patriotism, and willingness for sacrifice. Instead, it served as little more than a voyeuristic spectacle that appealed to the sadistic impulses of anti-Semites while offending the moral sensibilities of non-Nazi Germans.

The Winter Relief organization was aimed at improving the new regime's image by providing a positive demonstration of national and social solidarity, as well as a symbolic example of the Nazis' "socialism of deeds." Donations were collected on streets, in places of work, and by volunteers going door-to-door. Celebrities from the worlds of politics, economics, and culture were among those who pledged their time to raise money. Moreover, on one Sunday a month, the nation was called upon to make do with a simple "one-pot" meal instead of the traditional roast. All these measures combined to symbolize the eradication of class divides in German society. Solidarity and propaganda here merged into one, personified in the figure of Joseph Goebbels, who headed both the Ministry of Propaganda and the Ministry of Public Welfare. It was the practical realization of Harold Lasswell's dictum: "Gestures of condolence plus bread are far more potent than bread alone."[41]

While the parallels between the Blue Eagle campaign and the Winter Relief program extended even to the issuing of emblems to be worn by the participants, there was, of course, the major difference that in Germany violent repercussions from noncompliance were far more likely than in Roosevelt's America. For all the claims of "voluntary contributions," popular participation was enshrined in tax regulations, since the German tax authority automatically deducted 20 percent of workers' taxable incomes if they did not explicitly opt out of the contributions. Those who paid up were issued a monthly placard that exempted them from door-to-door solicitations. Those who did not could be fired on the spot, and although they could sue to regain their jobs, the legal route was risky. While the courts reaffirmed Germans' *de jure* right to nonparticipation in voluntary campaigns, judges *de facto* convicted recalcitrants of antisocial behavior toward the German *Volk*. One such conviction in 1937, for instance, found the plaintiff guilty of "gross misuse of the freedom accorded to him by the Führer in his confidence in [the essential goodness of] the German soul."[42]

Divergent as the New Deal and Nazism were when it came to application of direct state coercion, they were similar in their political rhetoric and the underlying psychology behind that rhetoric. Both operated in what historian Aryeh Unger has called, with reference to the Winter Relief program, the "vast and vaguely delimited no-man's-land of *voluntary compulsion*."[43]

WE CAN NOW distinguish between two forms or phases of mass propaganda. *Mobilizing propaganda*, if successful, activates a latent potential for public enthusiasm and approval. It is the media extension and the mass-reproduced voice of charismatic leadership. Yet like that charisma, it can remain effective for only a limited period of time. Once the initial excitement generated by charisma has ebbed, *maintenance propaganda*—which may be described as the workhorse of a regime's endeavors to control public opinion—is required to shore up support. In practice, of course, the two types of propaganda never occur in pure form. Roosevelt's fireside chats, the Blue Eagle campaign, and the Winter Relief program blended both types, with one or the other dominating according to situations and strategy. As the demise of "real existing socialism" shows, maintenance propaganda becomes lifeless, mind-deadening cant if it does not awaken at least a modicum of passion.

The dynamic set in motion by the Roosevelt administration and the Hitler regime in the summer and fall of 1933 provides a wonderful paradigm of propaganda's dual function of raising passions and then stabilizing them as part of everyday routines. The mood of activism unanimously identified by observers during the first months of both the New Deal and the Third Reich can only be understood as the attempt to jump-start a new spirit of "energy and enthusiasm,"[44] as John Maynard Keynes put it. Through the marches, parades, and issue campaigns; the rashes of legislation; the creation of ministries, agencies, special commissions, and mass organizations; as well as the introduction of public holidays, the new regimes made clear that they had actually created the new reality that previous governments merely proclaimed. Reporting on the first year of the Third Reich, a French observer asked, "Is there a precise political and economic program being put forth in all these mass demonstrations? It is doubtful. They seem to be exclusively about the awakening and maintenance of enthusiasm." His rhetorical question applied equally well to Roosevelt's New Deal.[45]

This is not to say that either National Socialism or the New Deal failed to communicate a political and economic agenda. On the contrary, there was no end to the proclamations by the Hitler regime and the Roosevelt administration about what they intended to do. But the actual content of those proclamations was secondary in importance to the gesture, which conveyed will, determination, strength, and dynamism. What captivated the public imagination was not any particular project and its chances for success but the emotional charge of how such projects were presented. In this context, the opportunism of both governments, so often emphasized by historians of Germany and the United States, appears in a new light. It is true that in both cases, reform programs aimed at ending the

Depression had been prepared by previous regimes.[46] But Herbert Hoover and Hitler's predecessors in Germany had utterly lacked the talent for theatricality, spectacle, fanfare, and communion with the masses. Too unimaginative and too powerless to offer a workable economic perspective, they were equally unable to come up with a soul-stirring propagandistic one—much like the German Social Democratic Party in its propaganda struggle against the Nazis. By contrast, National Socialism and the New Deal possessed the gift most necessary for political success in the 1930s: the ability to use symbols innovatively, confidently, and unscrupulously.[47]

The Propaganda Game

Ever since the Romans invented the formula of bread and circuses, the goal of propaganda has been to make the audience believe that it lives in the best of all possible worlds—or at least that it is on its way toward that promised land. This effect has been described simply and accurately as the "feel-good factor."[48] In times of material prosperity, the combination of the consumer and culture industries renders overt political propaganda largely superfluous. The stability of Western consumer societies during the 1920s and between the 1950s and 1990s was not so much the result of people's belief in freedom and democracy as a testimony to their prosperity. Conversely, political propaganda in the United States and Germany in the 1930s was able to mask the consumer crisis by conjuring up an astonishingly effective feel-good factor.

The New Deal took its name from a card-game metaphor,

and with that in mind, perhaps one could speak of it as a boldly successful bluff. The metaphor of games of chance specifically and games in general is as central to our understanding of the New Deal as is the analogy to war. Looking back on the Roosevelt administration, historians Thomas Vernor Smith and Warren Susman saw it as the epitome of "the great American game" of politics.[49] Fittingly, Roosevelt's secretary of labor, Frances Perkins, said of FDR: "He loved the game of politics, and has played it like a master." And Stuart Chase, the star political journalist and best-selling author who may have coined the phrase "New Deal," ended his 1932 book of that title with the question "Why should the Russians have all the fun of remaking a world?"[50] The idea that success is the result of exploiting one's chances, as in a game, is deeply embedded in the American unconscious. And the New Deal was *the* form of politics in a decade that saw games take on an unprecedented importance in society, becoming absolutely central to mass culture.

If we broaden the notion of games to include sports, which grew hugely in popularity during the 1930s, and leisure culture in general, it becomes apparent that this phenomenon does not so much reflect an actual increase in sporting and recreational activities as it does their closer connection with the state. The first great burgeoning of game, sports, and leisure culture occurred prior to World War I. During the 1920s, when the cult of the body was freed from the last remaining moral constraints of the Victorian era, sports were established as a mass pastime. What followed in the 1930s was the discovery, subsidization, and instrumentalization of this sphere by the state. The transformation occurred first and foremost in the totalitarian nations—for example, in the *dopolavoro* recreational clubs in Fascist Italy and the *Kraft durch Freude* (Strength Through Joy) program in the Third Reich. The liberal democracies later followed suit, not in the form of state-sponsored mass organizations but through the introduction of annual holidays for workers and state subsidies for tourism.

The New Deal, too, never attempted to nationalize the culture of sports and recreation; rather, as with most other domains, it left its organization to the private sector, local communities, and individual states. But the contours of this culture were determined by encouragement and subsidies from Washington: playgrounds and sports fields, public swimming pools and beaches, nature reserves and parks with picnic and camping areas, observation platforms, and outdoor amphitheaters were all part of what has been called "the New Deal landscape." That landscape also included the parkways, roads that wound along scenic routes and were intended, as was the autobahn in Germany, to encourage automotive tourism.

In support of his thesis about the centrality of games in the New Deal, and—in contrast to the totalitarian states—their civilizing effect, Warren Susman drew from the work of French theorist Roger Caillois. In Caillois's seminal study *Man, Play and Games*, we read:

> If the principles of play in effect correspond to powerful instincts . . . , it is readily understood that [these instincts] can be positively and creatively gratified only under ideal and circumscribed conditions, which in every case prevail in the rules of the game. Left to themselves, destructive and frantic as are all instincts, these basic impulses can hardly lead to any but disastrous consequences. *Games discipline instincts and institutionalize them.* For the time

that they afford formal and limited satisfaction, they edu-
cate, enrich, and immunize the mind against their viru-
lence. At the same time, they are made fit to contribute
usefully to the enrichment and the establishment of various patterns of culture [emphasis added].[51]

Among the "powerful instincts" Caillois cites is vertigo, the
condition of intoxicated trance one feels, for instance, after riding a carousel or a roller coaster. But Caillois also includes the
Nazi Party's mass rallies in Nuremberg, which he calls "orches-
trated vertigo."

One is tempted to add that the same holds true for all of the
programs and events organized under National Socialism and
the New Deal—different as they were—insofar as they were
aimed at keeping the populace on the move, in a state of intox-
ication but always under control. But before we explore this
issue, we must first explore how the spaces in which the production of vertigo was to take place were redefined and reorganized.

· 4 ·

BACK TO THE LAND

By 1933, nationalism was more than one hundred years old and had taken on a variety of forms and ideological shadings, ranging from the revolutionary Jacobinism of the late eighteenth century to the bourgeois, liberal version of the 1800s to later imperialist, philosophical, literary, and biological-racist variants. Its popularity rose and fell in cycles corresponding negatively to the popularity of its great adversary and alter ego, cosmopolitanism. The two were like a pair of dancers who constantly swapped the lead, with one partner taking over when the other grew tired.

In addition, nationalism was essentially a middle-class ideology. Its emergence coincided with the rise of the middle classes, the only segment of population that defined itself in terms of the nation and was willing to risk all for it. That identification meant that the middle classes were also subject to the ups and downs suffered by the ideology itself. No sooner had national ideals been realized in the wars of unification (the American Civil War, the Italian Risorgimento, and the German wars of 1866–71) than they were undermined by the unbridled capitalism of the periods that followed, only to be revived, almost half a century later, by the World War I generation, who, disgusted by their parents' materialism, threw themselves into an idealistic war they believed would purify the nation. The same cycle was repeated—in accelerated tempo—after World War I. The upsurge of idealism embodied in the "sacred union" of the Great War gave way to the materialistic hedonism of the Roaring Twenties; this, in turn, was followed by the collapse of the Great Depression and the rediscovery of the nation and its embodiment, the state, seen as the only real and reliable source of value and the last refuge in times of desperation. Just as the outbreak of World War I in 1914 pulled the rug out from under the certainty of lasting peace and prosperity, so the crash of 1929 was experienced as a plunge from a presumably permanent state of affluence and well-being into a bottomless void. The desire to recover some ground beneath one's feet—in an entirely literal as well as metaphorical sense—was the 1930s' most powerful collective psychological impulse. After 1929, the threat to the common welfare was seen as the inevitable result of international, free-market capitalism—a labile, accident-prone, uncontrollable, and irresponsible system. The search began for a more disciplined state, a new Sparta of sorts, in which the public welfare would not be based on illusion but firmly rooted in tangible reality.

In economics, that role had been previously played by the gold standard. Stored away like the mythic horde of the

Nibelungs in the central banks of the world's leading nations, gold had been the material "ground" guaranteeing the security and stability of national currencies, of which the gold coins in circulation until 1914 were the everyday physical manifestation. With the disappearance of those coins and the transfer of European reserves to the United States to pay for World War I, the gold standard no longer provided a sense of confidence in postwar Europe. Without gold reserves to back them up, people feared that national currencies would lose all weight, worth, and proportion. The value of money would randomly bob up and down, freed from restraints of gravity and lacking any sense of balance. Some attempts were made to restore the gold standard in the 1920s, before economic collapse permanently ended the age of gold in the early '30s.[1] The end of the liberal economy's foundation on gold triggered the search for new "ground." In Italy and Germany, and every other country affected by the Depression, the search generated the myth of the land: from a literal point of view, the soil on which man lived and which he cultivated with his hands; from an imaginative perspective, the newly discovered physical contours of the nation.

A corresponding process occurred in the psychology of politics. People no longer looked to liberal democracy, which they held responsible for the Depression, for protection and guidance. Instead, they placed their trust in a new type of authoritarian state, personified institutionally by Il Duce and the Führer in Italy and Germany, and symbolically by President Roosevelt in the United States. The cornerstone of the leader's legitimacy was the idea that he embodied the nation as a whole, and under his leadership, the course the nation was to pursue led not outward but inward. Economically, the leader's task was to emancipate the nation from the world economy and replant it in its native soil. Only on clearly delimited, finite, controllable ground, it was felt, could the nation begin to convalesce from the sickness of liberal internationalism. By 1939, political essayist Ferdinand Fried would conclude that for Germany the state itself had become the "replacement for the gold standard."[2]

Autarky, or national economic self-sufficiency, became the watchword of the 1930s, but this was more than just an economic concept. Fried, a radical conservative, neatly summed up a perspective shared by many of his contemporaries on both sides of the ideological spectrum:

> The powerful but ultimately accursed intoxication of freedom is a thing of the past. People have had to recognize their limits, and they are withdrawing in disappointment and dismay from the gambling table and all its swindles. They are becoming more contented and are again beginning to direct their lives and thoughts inward. . . . They've begun reflecting about the ground on which they stand, about the society into whose midst they've been placed, about family, tribe, and kinship between members of the German *Volk*. After a precipitous flight into freedom, they've found their way back to the ties forged by nature.[3]

The emphasis on economic autarky was not the only inward-looking tendency; 1930s nationalism was generally introverted and defensive. Even Fascism and National Socialism were, in their early years, disinclined toward aggressive expansion.

Before they set out on their bellicose adventures (Italy in 1935 and Germany in 1938), both regimes pursued a kind of "inner colonization," which took the form of what we today would call infrastructural improvement initiatives for underdeveloped areas.

In a strange analogy, the same was true in the Soviet Union, where 1924 had marked the end of proletarian internationalism and the idea of world revolution, just as 1929 marked the end of liberal capitalism in the West. Stalin's promulgation of "socialism in one country" effectively killed off Lenin and Trotsky's dream of communist internationalism. The Soviet-Russian nationalism that superceded the idea of a world revolution under Stalin was as autarkic, defensive, and introspective as the prevailing sentiments in pre-1937 Italy, Germany, and the United States.

THE NATION THAT was rediscovered in the 1930s was one of all the people. There were no classes, just ordinary citizens who united beyond their class divisions to form a community. The ideal reverberated in central phrases such as "the people" and "the common American" in the New Deal and in neologisms like "*Volk* comrade" or "*Volk* community" in National Socialism.[4] Strikingly, although the means they employed to deal with their opponents could hardly have been more different, both the New Deal and National Socialism used the same term, "plutocracy," to tar those they wanted to depict as the nation's enemies. While the New Deal portrayed itself as combating the financial metropolis of Wall Street and restoring

Washington as the seat of power emanating from the people, National Socialism depicted its confiscation of Jewish property as a long-overdue nationalization of native assets that had fallen into enemy hands.

Another parallel, this one with the Soviet Union, was the importance of show trials. New Deal Washington flexed its rejuvenated muscles in the form of numerous congressional investigative committees, before which putative enemies of the people—for example, wartime profiteers and stock market speculators—were called upon to answer for their actions. In the early 1930s, the Senate Committee on Banking and Currency trained its attention on those who had profited from the rampant stock market speculations of the 1920s, while the Senate Special Committee on Investigating the Munitions Industry concluded that the "merchants of death" had not only enriched themselves at the cost of the nation but had led the United States into war in the first place. The notorious Special House Committee on Un-American Activities (which later took a different political course) originated in these early attempts at pillorying supposed national enemies in popular tribunals.

Still, images of the enemy paled in importance to what the nation had to offer in a positive sense. From state-produced propaganda to state-financed public works projects, huge emphasis was placed on "nationalizing" the people along the lines of the famous dictum adapted by Italian Fascism from the Risorgimento: "After we've created Italy, the next task will be to create Italians." A major shortcoming of nineteenth-century nationalism, from the viewpoint of the 1930s, was that it had never proceeded beyond abstraction. Except for brief upsurges in patriotism during wartime, the people had maintained an emotional distance from the nation. In contrast, the new nation of the 1930s was to be not just a state but a true homeland.

Regionalism

The conventional assessment of Fascism and National Socialism is that the two movements were utterly unoriginal when it came to positive achievements for their respective peoples. While this view cannot be entirely dismissed, it should be revised since the same basically holds true for other political ideologies and regimes. Indeed, it would be difficult to find a single government that does not borrow liberally from the past. The Western democracies of the 1930s, and in particular America under the New Deal, would be unimaginable without imitation of previous models.

With Fascism, National Socialism, and the New Deal, we can draw a direct line from the state solutions put forward in the 1930s to reforms first suggested in the period 1890–1910. Conceived, planned, and in some cases implemented by a reformist minority, those ideas fell victim to World War I. In the aftermath of the war, none of the participants except the United States had the financial resources to undertake "luxury" reforms. Indeed, luxury reforms—attempts by highly developed societies at self-improvement—were exactly what the proposals two decades earlier had been. The common denominator among the various ideas in the various countries was the effort to restore some of the qualities of life that had been destroyed or seriously damaged by fifty (in Britain, one hundred) years of laissez-faire capitalism. They included proposals on how to lift the individual above the anonymous crowd, how to preserve a sense of community against free-market competition, how to revive artisanship in an age of cheap mass production, and how to rescue "organic culture" from empty, atomizing "civilization." The pioneers of this movement were thinkers as diverse as William Morris, Friedrich Nietzsche, and Hippolyte Taine, and the practical activism they inspired was just as varied, ranging from the Arts and Crafts movement in England and the United Workshops in Germany to guild socialism, corporatism, the country-house and garden-city movements, youth groups, experimental communes, societies for the preservation of natural and historic monuments, and American conservationism (which was led by Theodore Roosevelt).

Viewed as a whole, the reform initiatives were a contradictory mix of pre- and postcapitalist elements. They simultaneously looked back toward the medieval past, which was perceived as organic, protected, and socially intact, and toward a utopian future that reformers hoped to reach by imitating that past. If these efforts seem reactionary, then reactionaries made up a major portion of the progressive turn-of-the-century European intellectual elite, including the Marxist founder of English guild socialism, William Morris, and even Karl Marx himself.[5]

PART OF THIS back-to-the-future movement was the revival of "the region," in all its geographical, historical, cultural, social, biological, and mental particularity, as an older and more authentic notion of place than the relatively new concept of the nation. Not surprisingly, renewed interest in regions as the basic, "organic" units of which states are made up first arose in France, where over the course of three hundred years local cultures had been subjected to exceptionally intense pressure by the centralized national government. On the surface, the new regionalism would seem to contradict the nationalist and imperialist fascination with large, even global spaces that set the tone for the times. But in fact, the two outlooks complemented each other. Regionalism provided people with a clearly delineated sphere of existence to counteract the frightening sense of borderless, limitless space that accompanied imperialist expansion. France's transition, beginning in 1880, from a largely agrarian society to a global imperial power thus went hand in hand with the nostalgic ideology of native soil, or *les terres*, developed by thinkers such as Taine and Maurice Barrès. The idea of national identity being rooted in "blood and soil" was anything but a particularly German phenomenon. As much as its French, German, English, and American variants may have differed in both theory and practice, the cult of soil, land, and "organic" society at the end of the nineteenth century reflected an international desire to withdraw from the chill of modernity into the warmth of the regional and the local.

In and of itself, this desire was not necessarily reactionary, as the example of the homeland preservation, or *Heimatschutz*, movement in Wilhelmine Germany illustrates. The *Heimatschutz* movement began in 1904, ten years after the establishment of the National Trust of Historic Sites and Natural Scenery in Britain, upon which it was modeled. Its founders were enlightened conservatives. Far from being enemies of technology, these men were in fact convinced of the inevitability of technological and industrial development. They merely opposed the anarchism of laissez-faire development and sought to reconcile economic progress with the preservation of historically and culturally evolved landscapes. Paul Schultze-Naumburg, an architect and chairman of the committee that formed the first *Heimatschutz* association, shared a number of goals with William Morris and the Arts and Crafts movement, including the appreciation for organic materials, the respect for artisan skills, and the concern with the functionality and aesthetic quality of the item. Yet whereas the Arts and Crafts movement refused to compromise in any form with industry, the decidedly more modernist German preservationists accepted the necessity of industrial production while trying to ennoble it. The educated middle class that made up the movement's membership were a homogeneous group without any polarizing political-ideological camps. Conservatives like Schultze-Naumburg peacefully coexisted with modernists like Walter Gropius, later one of the founders of the Bauhaus. They also shared the basic conviction that modern architectural styles were to be both functional and aesthetically pleasing, and that they should harmonize with the cultural traditions of the society they were meant to serve.

All this changed drastically after 1918. With Germany's military and political collapse leading to a crisis in public morale, and with postwar inflation spelling ruin for the middle class, the prewar initiatives put forward by a flourishing bourgeois subculture became bitter bones of contention. Perhaps not since the decade prior to the French Revolution had so promising a reform movement been drawn so violently into political conflict. The defeated nations experienced this clash first and with the greatest intensity. But the winners had at most a grace period of a few years. The beginning of the Great Depression in 1929—or, more fittingly, the global economic collapse, or even the global defeat of liberal capitalism—signaled a state of emergency for the entire capitalist world. This collapse utterly undermined previous attempts to reform the liberal system. It was one thing to develop concepts for reform from the comfort of a secure environment—say, from one's thriving architecture studio in a suburban villa. It was something entirely different to ponder reform amid a crisis of the magnitude of the Great Depression. Economic ruin and existential anxiety split society into embittered political-ideological fronts. How an individual thought and acted was no longer his own personal affair but suddenly became, whether he liked it or not, part of the polarized political battle over the causes of and potential solutions to the global crisis.

So, for example, the politically neutral *Heimatstil* (native style) movement of prewar Germany was transformed into a reactionary chauvinistic agenda for ethnic purity in architecture: the pitched roof, or *Spitzdach*, of traditional German architecture against the flat roof, or *Flachdach*, of Bauhaus modernism. Other indications of this sea change include Schultze-Naumburg's membership in the Nazi Party, Le Corbusier's turn to *Heimatstil* in the 1930s, and his sympathy for the Vichy regime in the 1940s. After devoting himself in the 1920s to the urban idea of the *ville radieuse*, or "radiant city," Le Corbusier focused his attention in the 1930s on a form of organizing rural spaces he called the *ferme radieuse*, or "radiant farm."

As he himself described it, the *ferme radieuse* was "an integral part of the soil, of the region, of nature, and of human work." And on another occasion, in a complete reversal of his early views, Le Corbusier opined, "The cities are the corollary of the countryside—and not vice versa."[6]

THE FIN DE siècle generation, disenchanted with the industrial age, had, from its position of relative comfort, discovered and cultivated a vision of a preindustrial paradise. The generation of 1929, with far greater cause for disenchantment, grasped at those same ideas and proposals in the hope of finding a foothold to break their fall into the economic void. It is possible, of course, that the 1930s revival of ideas from 1900 was quite unconscious. Perhaps, like the desperate Scarlett O'Hara at the turning point in *Gone with the Wind*, people in the 1930s instinctively clutched at the ground, at their native soil, because it alone seemed to offer something reassuringly elemental and stable—in contrast to what Edmund Wilson called the "gigantic fraud" of pre-Depression prosperity.

However aware people in the 1930s were of their motivations, the new emphasis on soil in all its forms, from the farmer's field to the regional landscape, now took on quasi-religious, magical, "primordial" significance. The back-to-the-land movement was hardly the exclusive province of rabid blood-and-soil fanatics. Nazi minister of agriculture and notorious blood-and-soil ideologue Richard Walther Darré succeeded in attracting a mass following for his idiosyncratic notions only because they reflected the spirit of the times. And Franklin D. Roosevelt was also among those for whom the soil was like a magic substance that would miraculously regenerate a world devastated by capitalism.

The adherents of this new cult ranged from militant anti-industrialists, who demanded the complete reagriculturalization of society, to representatives of the most technologically advanced sectors of modern industry. Henry Ford, for instance, repeatedly stressed the need for equilibrium between industry and agriculture. "With one foot in agriculture and one foot in industry," Ford told an interviewer, "America is safe." He supported the breakup of large industrial complexes and their relocation to rural areas. In a 1933 interview with the *Christian Science Monitor*, Ford unveiled a plan for linking soybean and automobile production:

> The farmer grows the legume and I pay him for it. Moreover, he will do the initial processing that fits it for industrial use, and I shall pay him for it. I shall use the oil to make paint and enamel and the other substances in the bean to make parts for the car, and he will buy my car, which uses the bean that grows on his land.

This inspired a German commentator to write of Ford's vision of "cars sprouting from fields."[7]

Germany and the United States—the world's two most advanced industrialized nations, and the two hardest hit by the Depression—both toyed with the idea of decentralization to "roll back" industrial concentration. Among the proposals put forward by experts such as Germany's Egon Bandmann were the "de-rationalization" and "de-Taylorization" of the economy. Stuart Chase suggested imposing a ten-year moratorium on technological and organizational innovation, arguing that innovation had led to the erratic prosperity of the 1920s and to the Depression.

A year before writing *The New Deal*, Chase was already singing the praises of preindustrial happiness and contentment in Mexican society.[8] In his book *Mexico: A Study of Two Americas* (1931), a best seller based on his personal experience of life beyond the Rio Grande, Chase advised Americans to emulate their southern neighbors:

> The handicraft economy of Mexico is economically stable and self-sufficient. There are no rich, no poor, no paupers, no sexual inhibitions beyond the reasonable tolerant folkways. There is no local government worthy of the name, but a strong community spirit, finding expression not in after-dinner speeches and paid advertisements, but in helping a neighbor harvest his corn, and repairing the town water supply. In such communities, pecuniary standards do not apply, and integrity is not a luxury. Men are governed not by clocks but by the sun and the seasons; recreation is not a matter of paid admissions or forced disciplines, but as spontaneous as eating. The individual to survive must learn many useful crafts; he does not atrophy his personality by specializing in one. Costs are lower for many articles than is conceivable under the most efficient methods of mass production, and all work is directed to specific functions with a maximum economy and a minimum of waste. Overproduction is as unthinkable as unemployment. Life in a handicraft community is to be lived, not to be argued about.[9]

Elegies like these, though infused with the romantic image of noble savages happily thriving in a kind of ur-Communist harmony, were more than just bucolic fantasies set, as they were, against the backdrop of the ongoing crisis that gave rise to them. The way out of the Depression, in the view of men like Chase, was to create a new synthesis of modern technology and "humane," preindustrial culture—by, for example, putting electricity to work for artisans and small, decentralized, quasi-artisan industry. To adapt the Mexican model to the United States, Chase advocated "small plants in the open country fed by cheap electric power, where workers have each his truck garden. . . . Electric lights, small motors, power-driven tools can aid potters, weavers, leather workers, silversmiths." Decentralization, he argued, was ideal for "maintaining and encouraging the handicrafts."[10] It would be an interesting topic for further research to investigate just how many of the preachers of modernity of the 1920s became regional traditionalists during the Depression, following the example of Le Corbusier, who encouraged his fellow citizens to return "to our resuscitated and revived Mother Earth."[11]

The goal was thus to restore the balance and harmony between nature and the economy, and between technology and culture, which many believed had been destroyed during the nineteenth century. The ideas put forward revolved around the question of how to reorganize a bloated—and busted—economy of big, consolidated industrial and agricultural concerns into a more modest, well-rounded, and, above all, crisis-resistant system. The solution, it was thought, lay in returning to the "organic" mixed production of earlier times. That entailed "reagriculturalization," or the breaking down of large-scale industry into smaller units that would be embedded within or otherwise interwoven with agricultural production. The idea was like a nonpunitive version of the Morgenthau Plan, the proposal floated during World War II that would have eradicated heavy industry in post-Nazi Germany and

turned the country back into an agrarian state. Reagriculturalization was both a short- and a long-term concept; it sought
at once to overcome the concrete problems of the Depression
and to create a social utopia for future generations. First, on
the unemployment front, the jobless were to be set up as subsistence farmers who would occasionally, as the economy
demanded, leave their plots of land to work in small, local
factories. Second, by reversing the trend toward ever more specialized labor, a new economic culture would be created—
indeed a revolutionary culture in general—in which a new type
of "organic" citizen (in contrast to the mechanized workers of
the industrial age) would live and work. Third, because the system was autarkic, so the logic ran, it would be automatically
resistant to future world economic crises.

Regionalism played a double role in this doctrine of salvation as both a normative environmental philosophy and a strategy for realizing that ideal in specific local areas. Both National
Socialism and the New Deal devoted unprecedented energy to
regional planning. In so doing they institutionalized and instru-
mentalized what had been in the 1920s a marginal, fledgling
academic discipline. Interestingly, in the early years of the
Third Reich, regionalism as a science proceeded pretty much
without government interference. That relative autonomy was
revoked once the war began.[12]

IN A SHARED bit of rhetoric and ideology, National Socialism, Fascism, and the New Deal all depicted their rise to power
as the concrete realization of the idea of the nation, which until
then had been unformed, halfhearted, and theoretical. At best

the nation had been a "mechanical" or "artificial" construct, an arbitrary state, riddled with class divisions, that had failed to incorporate and engage the whole population and thus lacked the legitimate basis of either the people or the soil. In Germany, the tropes of "people" and "soil" were, of course, inflected with racist ideas of blood. Konrad Meyer, one of the leading regional planners, defined the mission of his discipline thus: "to explore and evaluate German territory in all its varieties as the fundament of the German *Volk*, . . . with the aim of illuminating the indivisible connection between the land and the life and greatness of this people, so that this deeper understanding of the power of the land provides a solid, practical basis for the National-Socialist renewal of the German empire." In another passage, he defined his primary task as "directing research toward the true wellsprings of our national life: *the German people and its need for Lebensraum, blood and soil.*"[13]

If we translate specifically Nazi phrases like "blood and soil" into what were at the time internationally popular concepts of organic authenticity, Meyer's statements would not diverge all that much from opinions held by liberal American adherents of regionalism. Lewis Mumford, for example, defined regionalism as "an effort which recognizes the existence of real groups and social configurations and geographic relationships that are ignored by the abstract culture of the metropolis and which opposes the aimless nomadism of modern commercial enterprise with the conception of a stable and settled and balanced and cultivated life."[14]

American regionalists also emphasized the role of the region in giving the nation an "organic" coherence, replacing the "mechanical" pseudocommunity of the liberal age. Burdett G.

Lewis, for instance, wrote, "Regionalism strikes an effective and natural medium between uncontrolled individualism among the states and complete centralization of administration in Washington." Meanwhile, Mumford asserted that regional planning

> sees people, industry and the land as a single unit ... it means the reinvigoration and rehabilitation of whole regions so that the products of culture and civilization, instead of being confined to a prosperous minority in the congested centers, shall be available to everyone at every point.

Sociologist Howard W. Odum concurred:

> Far from being a panacea for the artificial reconstruction of the nation ... [regionalism] is the most natural thing in the world ... pointing equally to the past or future. It assumes the totality of all environmental factors of nature and of all cultural factors. ... [It is a] tool and technique for various objectives of planning and of attaining equilibrium and balance, decentralization and distribution, in particular as these relate to population, to wealth and to sovereignty.

To invoke the title of the final chapter in Odum's book, regionalism was nothing less than the straightest and most smoothly paved path "towards national integration."[15]

The advocates of regionalism made no bones about the fact that their vision of national renewal, if realized, would have serious consequences for the founding document of United States democracy. Odum argued for the necessity of "re-examining the Constitution," while Harvard professor of government William

Yandell Elliott openly speculated in 1935 about the judicial possibility of reconstituting the United States into "regional commonwealths" that would replace the federal states.[16]

Such ruminations should obviously not be put on a par with the National Socialist regime's actual eradication of the federal states that made up pre-1933 Germany and its reorganization of the country into districts run by party leaders. It is conceivable, however, that the discussions within the Nazi Party that led to this drastic reorganization featured arguments similar to those made by the American regionalists.

In Germany, as elsewhere, it was never in fact the idealists and theorists of autonomy and diversity who were charged with turning their notions into reality; on the ground, technocrats and planners took over. That was made clear in one of the main efforts to give the regional principle a stable basis: the attempt to create a self-sufficient and viable territorial unit.

The Settlement

Around 1900, the settlement* joined the city and the village as a third, hybrid form of communal residence. A product of the reform movements of the time, it was neither strictly urban nor strictly rural. Inspired by the Rousseauian ideal of modest scale, it combined elements of both into a new synthesis. The settlement was a relatively small community inhabited by a

---

*The German term *Siedlung* refers to a suburban form for which there is no English equivalent. It incorporates both the idea of the garden city and the homestead, as well as the notion of community. The English term "settlement" best covers all these meanings.

limited number of people who would ideally be connected by a greater common interest than was usual among either tenants or individual home owners. As a social project, the settlement aimed to transcend the perennial conflicts—between town and country, industry and agriculture, living and working—by creating a qualitatively new set of "organic" hybrid relationships.

In 1898, Britain's Ebenezer Howard published a book entitled *To-morrow: A Peaceful Path Toward Real Reform*, in which he set out a conceptual plan for what he called "garden cities." From the 1910s, when the first attempts were made to put Howard's ideas into practice, to the 1970s, when the movement finally petered out, Howard's "garden cities" exerted enormous influence on modern architecture's attempts to create towns that were planned, pleasant, and green. Significantly, Howard and his successors' focus was on changing the city, and their main goal was to connect urban areas with the countryside or, perhaps more precisely, to endow urban life with rural qualities. Upon closer inspection, the planned cities of Howard, Frank Lloyd Wright, and Le Corbusier amount to conglomerations of individual settlements, which were distinguished from the sprawling sea of houses of the liberal age by their order, their organization, and their green spaces. As much as city and settlement planning often converged around the turn of the century, it was always the settlement, not the city, that provided the inspiration for change. Just as colonies often influence their mother nations, the settlement may be said to have infiltrated the city.

Still, for all its influence, the settlement movement prior to 1914 achieved its ideal of city-country synthesis only in the

sense of "greening" the urban space. The broader reconcilia-
tion between life and work, industry and agriculture to which
Howard aspired was dismissed as utopian "garden-city socialism."[17] There were only a few model projects, such as the
Hellerau settlement, near Dresden, that aimed to realize
Howard's ideal. Yet even Hellerau sidestepped the challenge of
merging factory or office labor with settlement living: those
who worked in Hellerau did so in privileged fields such as art,
handicrafts, architecture, music, or dance.

World War I gave the settlement movement new impetus
and direction, taking it further away from the ideal rural-urban
synthesis. First, the needs of war required the planning and
construction of housing for workers employed in the arma-
ments industry. In Europe as in the United States, the settlements sprouting up near centers of wartime production provided
a major impulse for postwar development. The second stage of
this reorientation took place after the war, primarily in those
European nations that had been defeated and impoverished—
with the highest degree of consistency in Germany. There, the
settlement movement abandoned the costly ideal of the garden
city in favor of more affordable housing blocks and development
complexes. The goal was no longer to achieve the "organic"
integration of city and nature but to fulfill the "functional"
requirements of urban living. German settlements between
1919 and 1929 were built on the urban periphery, where, to be
sure, there was lots of green; but the locations were not chosen
in order to realize a synthesis of town and country. Rather, the
green was reduced to being a functional element of the "urban
machine," the "green lung" on which the city depended as the
automobile depends on gasoline. When urban planners and

architects said, as they often did in the 1920s, that they wanted to produce houses the same way that Henry Ford produced cars, they were speaking more literally than figuratively.

Then came the collapse. The Great Depression buried the urban-functional ideal of the settlement, much as fifteen years previously World War I had interrupted Howard's vision of garden cities. Yet just as earthquakes often uncover hidden remnants of the past, the crisis triggered a reworked garden-city concept as an option for coping with the ongoing economic problems. The development was similar to the 1930s revival of turn-of-the-century regionalism under new and far more urgent circumstances. Whereas the pre-1914 settlement movement had articulated its critique of liberalism and its concept of town-country synthesis from a vantage point of material and existential security, the settlement movement of the 1930s was a direct response to economic and existential crisis. Its proponents were no longer reclining comfortably in their leather chairs. They were now arguing with their backs against the wall.

Subsistence Homesteads

The governments that immediately preceded National Socialism and the New Deal had already envisioned a type of settlement that seemed tailor-made to the new economic situation. Between 1930 and 1932, there were many proposals to move the jobless out of urban industrial centers as a means of relieving their suffering and containing the resulting social and political threat. The focus of the relocation was on the periphery of the cities, where the unemployed had already begun squatting of their own accord. The idea was to convert these unofficial "colonies" into state-subsidized and regulated settlements.

What was novel here was the idea that families would not only get a roof over their heads but a bit of land to cultivate so that they could feed themselves. The advantage for the state was that it would save money on welfare payments while defusing potentially explosive dissatisfaction among the jobless masses. The unemployed could be temporarily encamped in a quasi-rural, suburban cordon sanitaire, where they would wait for the economic crisis to pass and then be reintegrated into the labor market. Another advantage of this type of settlement was that it encouraged a new flexibility. Equally qualified for the assembly line and the subsistence garden, the worker-farmer was always employable, even if industry showed signs of only a partial recovery.

In this regard, what began as merely a means of dealing with a pressing crisis shaded over into a utopian vision of a new, crisis-resistant synthesis of town and country, industry and idyll. The willingness, indeed the need to believe in such visions, surfaced in all the industrialized nations in the 1930s.[18] Fascism, National Socialism, and the New Deal all made the garden-settlement into a cornerstone of their plans for a new form of civilization, feeding popular enthusiasm with appealing words, images, and projects.

IN THE FIRST hundred days of the New Deal, the Roosevelt administration prioritized its settlement program as one of its most important measures for combating the economic crisis and established a new governmental authority, the Subsistence Homesteads Division of the Department of Interior, to administer and realize the initiative. A subsistence homestead, according to the official definition, consisted "of a modern but inexpensive house and outbuildings, located on a plot of land upon which a family may produce a considerable portion of the food required for home consumption."

The typical subsistence homestead settlement encompassed twenty-five to three hundred such units, ranging in size between one and five acres, and included fruit and vegetable gardens, chickens, a pig, and, in some cases, a cow. The government was responsible for planning, financing, and building each project up until the very moment when the keys were handed over to the occupants. Tenants were given a thirty-year mortgage at 4 percent annual interest so that they would eventually be able to own the property.

The program was aimed not at the absolutely destitute but at the semiunemployed, whom the government wanted to save from abject poverty. A condition for participation in the program was that the prospective homesteader earn enough to meet his financial obligations. Self-sufficient farming was envisioned as a means for making up for decreased, lost, or intermittent income. Government thinking regarding farmers suffering from the consequences of agricultural overproduction ran along similar lines. The idea was to reorient their production to focus solely on their own personal needs and so free them for available work in factories—to "industrialize" farmers, much like the effort to "ruralize" factory workers. The ultimate goal was to create what Roosevelt termed "rural-urban industry," which would be crisis-proof and crisis-resistant.

Work on the first subsistence homestead project, Arthurdale, in West Virginia, began in the summer of 1933. Construction was finished within a few months, at which point the new houses were handed over—with considerable publicity—to several hundred unemployed miners and their families. Because the region lacked any industrial facilities, a small factory was also built. One of the intentions, as described by historian Paul Conkin, was to create a new model for small-town America.

> From their huts clinging to the hillside, from their lack of sanitary facilities, from the midst of malnutrition, disease, alcoholism, crime, delinquency, and high mortality, a fortunate few were to escape to pretty white homes, situated on small plots of farm land, surrounded by lawns, flowers, orchards, and fields. They were to enjoy regular meals, not through the bitter bread of charity, but through the food produced by their own hands. They were to have cows, poultry, root cellars, preserve closets, and plenty of air and sunshine. . . . They were to have partial employment in a government-sponsored post office factory, were to govern themselves through a town meeting, and were to find other sources of employment and a constructive use of leisure time in multiple handicrafts. The community was to point the way to a new way of life, not just for the miners, but for all America.[19]

Arthurdale was not a realistic program for alleviating extreme need but a propagandistic showpiece replete with state-sponsored jobs. Its geographical proximity to Washington, and in particular to the White House, was no accident, and much to the dismay of the responsible authorities, Eleanor Roosevelt and Roosevelt confidant Louis Howe often intervened in its

The Arthurdale settlement in West Virginia

planning and construction. They commissioned the architects, decided on the type of houses and gardens, chose the interiors, and made sure that Arthurdale got the sort of progressive school that would have been the envy of Newport, Rhode Island, or Westchester County, New York. (John Dewey and the dean of Teachers College at Columbia University were enlisted for the planning committee.)[20] Yet because the propagandistic intent of the project was all too apparent, its effect on public opinion was the opposite of what Roosevelt had intended. Ordinary America did not hail Arthurdale as a breakthrough. Instead, the project was criticized as an example of pie-in-the-sky government planning and bureaucratic waste.

This rocky start was one reason why the Subsistence Homesteads Division was dissolved in 1935, before the majority of its thirty-four projects had been completed, and its responsibilities

Children at play in Arthurdale

transferred to the newly founded Resettlement Administration. The idea of a mixed agrarian-industrial economy disappeared from the spotlight as quickly as it had appeared. With three exceptions (to which we will later return), the sixty projects realized before the resettlement program was canceled at the end of the decade were aimed simply at alleviating emergency situations and involved no grand social visions. Adherents continued to argue passionately for the idea, among them an Oklahoma congressman who urged that the budget for the subsistence homestead program be increased from $25 million to $4 billion, characterizing it as the only way out of the Depression and declaiming that otherwise "we are all lost."[21] For some social planners and reformers, including M. L. Wilson, founding director of the Subsistence Homestead Division, the program remained what it had been in its initial days: a laboratory for utopian experiments. But mainstream America, insofar as it took any notice of the post-Arthurdale settlements, and in particular the new communities' residents, mistrusted and opposed the planners' attempts to develop collective and cooperative forms of life. These were perceived as authoritarian and un-American, contrary to such values as individualism and competition. It may have been hyperbolic political rhetoric when a Roosevelt opponent described the settlement projects as "the first Soviet *colchos* on American soil." But it was another matter entirely when the homesteaders themselves complained about state regulation and regimentation, which in the eyes of many of them amounted to government control of their private lives. As historian Diane Ghirardo concludes, "settlers rightly felt that they were surrendering entirely too much freedom simply to obtain a loan or to remain on a project, and some felt that they were being spied upon, and that their privacy was unreasonably invaded." In this respect, the New Deal's homesteads not only resembled but outdid their equivalents in Mussolini's Italy.[22]

IN NATIONAL SOCIALIST Germany a "Reich Commission for Settlement Projects" was established soon after Hitler took power in 1933, and it was headed by the man one historian calls the embodiment of Nazi "middle-class socialism."[23] Gottfried Feder had written the first Party platform, with its prominent demand for the disempowerment of finance capital, which he called the "eradication of interest slavery." Feder later developed a concept, aimed at combating the Depression, of "productive exploitation of credit" that unwittingly approximated Keynesian deficit spending. Like M. L. Wilson in Washington,

Feder was a trained engineer. Perhaps that background explains his conviction that the only way to achieve a balanced "organic" society—in National-Socialist terms, "a *Volk* community"—was through medium-sized and, above all, decentralized industry. Feder advocated breaking up major banks and replacing centralized energy plants with regional, small and medium-sized facilities organized along cooperative lines. He also wanted to scale back the size of cities and relocate people to smaller settlement units. His ideal was the *Landstadt*, or "rural city," of no more than twenty thousand inhabitants, who would earn their living from agriculture, light industry, and artisan work. "Reconnection with the land" and "rural domestication" were Feder's alternatives to the construction of emergency housing for the unemployed during the Weimar Republic, and to achieve those aims, he planned to build one thousand *Landstädte* across Germany.[24]

None of his plans were completed or even begun. In 1934, Feder was dismissed from the post of Reich commissioner and stripped of all power within the party. Nonetheless, under his successor, J. W. Ludowici, also an advocate of the *Landstadt* concept, settlements remained a main pillar of National Socialist ideology and propaganda. The Nazi equivalent of Arthurdale was the showpiece settlement in Ramersdorf, near Munich, and the early Hitler regime promised that within a generation it would create space for some four million settlers, at a rate of one hundred to two hundred thousand annually. In reality, the construction undertaken between 1933 and 1936 failed to match that of the Weimar government from 1931 to 1932. The settlement program of the Third Reich no more represented a great leap forward than did the subsistence homesteads of the

The model town of Ramersdorf under construction

New Deal. Its main achievement was in the realm of propaganda, and even that did not last for more than a handful of years. As was the case with the New Deal, the department founded in 1933 to manage the settlements was disbanded, and its responsibilities transferred to a new agency.

The reason for the decline in the settlement projects in both Germany and the United States was that by 1936 middle-class-socialist hostility toward capitalism and industrial giants had ebbed—taking with it the widespread conviction that the best way out of the Depression was to scale back industry, reruralize the masses, and decentralize production. Men like M. L. Wilson and Gottfried Feder were shunted off into academic posts. In their wake, government policy was determined by others who were convinced that the solution lay not in breaking up but in streamlining industrial society.

One of the main American streamliners, M. L. Wilson's successor, Rexford Tugwell, believed that there was no way to reverse the processes of industrialization and urbanization and considered all attempts to return to idyllic preindustrial times mere tilting at windmills. Under his leadership, the settlement program abandoned the idea of the autarkic worker-farmer hybrid and harkened back to the earlier concept of the garden city. The three thousand "greenbelt towns" Tugwell envisioned, however, had little in common with Howard's ideas other than the presence of green spaces. They were not conceived as independent units where people lived and worked but as residential belt communities laid out as supplements to existing industrial centers. The greenbelt towns established near Washington, D.C., Cincinnati, and Milwaukee were purely residential areas for people who worked in those cities. To be sure, the locations were green; communal property was maintained to prevent real estate speculation; public amenities like community centers and sports facilities were built; and rents were controlled so as to be affordable to low-income families. Yet an essential element of Howard's ideal—the community as a true alternative to the city—was missing. Tugwell's greenbelt community was less an imitation of the English model than, as Tugwell himself said, the result of "some studies of our own town population movements, which showed steady growth in the periphery of cities. This contrasted with less growth or with actual losses both in rural areas and in metropolitan centers. In other words, it accepted a trend instead of trying to reverse it."[25]

Tugwell's plans met no more success than Feder's had. Of the three thousand greenbelt towns planned, only the three mentioned above were actually built. Like Arthurdale and the model projects of the Third Reich, they served primarily as showplaces. Nonetheless, Tugwell's model of bedroom communities on the periphery of cities did anticipate American suburbia as it developed after World War II.

In Germany, the stabilization of the economy and the beginning of the country's rearmament in 1936 marked a return to the old model of factory settlements, though with some modernist elements. Feder's idyllic *Landstadt* was superceded by the *Industrie-Gartenstadt*—well-organized residential areas, with lots of green but tied to large-scale industry. The best example of this sort of "industrial garden city" is Wolfsburg, the medium-sized town that was founded to provide a home for the newly established Volkswagen automobile concern and its workers.[26]

THE SHORT-LIVED infatuation with autarkic settlements and the ideal of the *Landstadt* would seem to suggest a victory of the realists over the utopians, which would indicate in turn that the New Deal and the Nazi regime were safely in the hands of social "real politicians." But that is not entirely the case. In retrospect, it is astonishing that what looks to us like a hopelessly anachronistic enterprise could occupy such a central position in the initial period of both the New Deal and National Socialism. For people in the early 1930s, however, the idea of scaling back industry, reagrarianizing the country, and decentralizing society did not seem like a pipe dream. The industrial revolution in Germany and the United States was a relatively recent historical event, only two generations in the past. Given its relative youth, industrialization had no claim to irreversibility. On the contrary, it seemed to some extent natural to ask whether industrialization might not have been a huge mistake. The popularity of the back-to-the-land slogans signal how vivid the memories of preindustrial existence must still have been.

Propaganda is successful when it picks up existing ideas, opinions, and desires and transforms them into a message of salvation. For the early years of the Roosevelt administration and the Hitler regime, visions of reconciling industry, cities, and the countryside—even in the seemingly mundane, non-heroic guise of settlements—were well suited for this purpose. The underlying utopian ideals elevated the settlement, giving it an inspiring, symbolic aura. As National Socialist propagandists knew, and as Gottfried Feder wrote in 1934 in the architectural journal he edited, the symbol was "the most objective and effective means of education, one which has thus far been fully appreciated and exploited only by the churches." In that sense, the new settlements might have become *the* symbol of National Socialist architecture. As Clemens J. Neumann wrote in Feder's publication, the settlements were, "in their purity and simplicity, in their unity of architectural form and intellectual standpoint, witnesses to a new collective spirit among the German *Volk*, bulwarks of communal solidarity."[27]

But in the long run, the settlements turned out not to possess the necessary symbolic power to fulfill this role. Whether in democracies or dictatorships, public housing simply lacks the grandeur to compete against prestige projects such as opera houses and the like—which is why, after 1936, propaganda began concentrating on other sorts of construction. Hitler explained the rationale behind the policy switch in a conversation with Hermann Rauschning:

> My buildings are a visible manifestation of the will to order that I convey to my people. My will is transmitted to the individual through the building. We are dependent upon the spaces in which we work and live. The people can measure the greatness and purity of our will in the greatness and purity of our architecture. Settlements and housing for workers would be absolutely the wrong place for me to begin. All of that will come—as a matter of course. But such things could have been achieved by a Marxist or bourgeois government. We alone as a party are capable of working—in freedom and strength—on the noblest of all art forms. Since the time of the medieval cathedrals, we are the first to make renewed demands on the artist for great, bold works. Let's have no modest homesteads or little houses, only the most massive projects since ancient Egypt and Babylon.[28]

Despite Hitler's claims to historical inspiration, in actual practice the architectural monumentalism of the Third Reich did not pattern itself after ancient Egyptian or Babylonian models. Instead, it looked toward the gigantic projects that had been undertaken in the Soviet Union a few years before. It was an orientation National Socialism shared with both Fascism and the New Deal.

· 5 ·

PUBLIC WORKS

All political systems have showcase projects through which they present themselves to the world and expect their aims, methods, and ideals to be judged. For Fascism, the New Deal, and National Socialism, those projects were, respectively, the reclamation of an area of swamplands, the building of dams and power plants along a forgotten river valley, and the construction of a national network of highways. To understand why these projects were so important to the three governments in question, we must first turn to the regime they all implicitly copied and competed against: the Soviet Union.

With its doctrine of world revolution, Soviet Communism had for the better part of a decade inspired widespread anxiety and fear in the capitalist West, while at the same time fascinating a radical, intellectual minority. In 1924, it suffered its first defeat: as capitalist nations recovered from the effects of World

War I, the global market was restabilized, and the potential for world revolution throttled. Following a protracted power struggle after Lenin's death in 1924, Stalin transformed the internationalist legacy of the Soviet Union into the idea of "socialism in one country." His vision was, so to speak, a kind of Russian "national socialism."

Stalin's rationale was simple. In order to face its enemies as an equal combatant and territorial superpower, if no longer the font of world revolution, the Soviet Union needed an economic base adequate to those aspirations. The foremost aim of "socialism in one country" was to allow the Soviet Union to catch up with the industrial revolution. This was not, in the eyes of Stalinist ideologues, an instance of slavishly imitating the West; nor was the industrialization of Russia intended to follow the classical model of Marx and Engels, with all its attendant agonies. On the contrary, in both form and scope the project was to be a unique event in world history—the complete transformation of society in one heroic fell swoop. Stalin's first Five-Year Plan for the Soviet economy proceeded less in the spirit of Lenin than as an act of Nietzschean will, or what historian Bernice Glatzer Rosenthal calls "Dionysian collectivism."[1] The plan's first major project, the damming of the Dnieper River and the construction of a massive power plant in 1927, represented a politically and psychologically astute gambit. It cast Stalin as a genuine successor to Lenin, a leader capable of realizing the latter's promise to bring electricity to the people ("Soviet power plus electrification equals Communism"), which had been made as part of the second party program in 1920 but never fulfilled. To commence Russia's industrialization with electrification meant having the benefit of state-of-the-art technology, which Western nations had perfected only after exhausting themselves with less advanced systems. From a propaganda perspective, there was hardly a more advantageous place to start, either in terms of the incipient battle for supremacy between Communism and capitalism or in terms of winning over the Soviet masses.

Stalin's first Five-Year Plan was inaugurated and accompanied by a propaganda machine fittingly called "Communism's dream factory." It consisted of two coordinated strategies: one was to depict the golden age of Communism to come; the other was to portray the heroic character of the work effort undertaken to reach that age. The subject of the propaganda was not only the work involved but the projects themselves. Never before had materials and objects such as cement and steel, backhoes and tractors, smokestacks and dams, power lines and turbines been treated with such epic, mythological grandeur. For the first time, mass-media techniques from capitalist advertising and escapist entertainment were applied to the purportedly soon-to-be-realized Soviet utopia of labor, technology, and "national socialist" progress.

In 1927, the West was too caught up in enjoying its own prosperity to take much note of events in Stalinist Russia. Contemporaries viewed Stalin's Five-Year Plan as a distant, exotic event consisting of statistical smoke and mirrors and pie-in-the-sky technological romanticism. It was a plan for a millennium and an attempt to hypnotize the masses with astronomic numbers—in other words, pure fantasy. In his 1931 book on Russia, Hans Siemsen dismissed the plan as a bit of unintentional comedy that might succeed in making Soviet citizens feel more "cheerful" but would do nothing to actually better their lot.[2] Only a minority of engineers, Marxists, and romantic revolutionaries took any serious interest in projects such as the Dnieper dam or the construction of the city of Magnitogorsk to serve a steel plant on the Ural River.

The West's sudden plunge from the Roaring Twenties into the Great Depression changed that attitude. Nowhere did the contrast between the two systems emerge more clearly than in the illustrated magazines showing unemployment lines and defunct factories in the older industrialized nations, as opposed to the beehive flurry of activity in the newly founded Soviet Union. Suddenly, the events in Russia no longer appeared remote and irrelevant to the West. They became the subject of widespread public interest—and imitation.

Although Mussolini's Fascism was the first regime in the West to gain power as an alternative to and counterrevolutionary bulwark against Bolshevism, it was also the first to learn lessons from Soviet Communism. Intellectuals and technocrats in Italy—in contrast to their German counterparts—followed the social and economic innovations of the Soviet Union with great interest until well into the 1930s. The Fascists were willing, indeed eager to compare their own order with the Soviet system, weighing the advantages and drawbacks. Newspapers and journals devoted just as much attention to the Soviet Union as they did to America, and authors such as Curzio Malaparte, Luigi Barzini, and Giacomo Gandolfi traveled to Russia and reported back positively about their experiences. While never questioning Fascism's fundamental historical superiority, these writers described what they saw in objective, thorough, and nonpolemical fashion, and their reports are full of respect for Soviet achievements. Italian Fascists treated Soviet Communism, much as they did the New Deal, as a step in the right direction—but one that Fascism had taken with greater consistency and determination. Communism was acknowledged as a post- and antiliberal system, lacking only the decisive Fascist insight that the triumph over free-market chaos depended not on the proletariat but on the nation.

Italians' interest in the Soviet Union also stemmed from the fact that both Russia and Italy lagged behind other Western nations in technological development. Italy may have considered itself culturally superior to "Asiatic" Russia, but it had to admit that it was not part of the industrial West. In 1930, three years after Stalin unveiled the Soviet plan to dam the Dnieper River, a gigantic act of subjugating untamed nature, Mussolini inaugurated a similar prestige project for his own regime.

The Agro Pontino

Once a productive farming region, the Pontine Marshes—a vast swampland some thirty minutes by train southeast of Rome—had long been an uninhabitable wasteland. Since the fall of the Roman Empire, various papal and secular authorities had tried to reclaim it without success. The project had become a symbol of Italian incompetence. The marshes formed a thirty-mile long and on average ten-mile wide rectangle, extending between the Alban Hills, the Lepini Mountains, and the Tyrrhenian Sea. With a total area of just over three hundred square miles, the marshland was about the size of greater Berlin. Depending on the time of year, it had a population of a few hundred to about a thousand people, largely shepherds, vagrants, seasonal laborers, and bandits, who lived, contemporary travelogues reported, under the most primitive conditions. Their reed huts reminded many observers more of African kraals than European houses, and the inhabitants were regarded less as Italians than as curious remnants of a prehistoric age. They were "desperate creatures, like missing links who eked out their existence in cohabitation with animals," said the journal *Civiltà fascista*, retrospectively describing them three years after the reclamation project was begun. "The *agro* was considered, like certain areas of Africa and America, an utter wilderness."[3]

Following the example of preceding governments, the Fascists, upon taking power, routinely promised as part of their program of national renewal to heal what they called the "festering wound at the heart of the nation."[4] During the first years of their rule, they put no more time or energy into the endeavor than any of their predecessors had. But the promise was revived and taken seriously when the Depression hit Italy in 1930. Mussolini had laid the groundwork two years earlier with the *bonifica integrale* land-improvement law. In contrast to the sort of legislation dealing with land reclamation, the *bonifica integrale* concerned not only the technological and physical improvement or reclamation of underutilized land; it aimed at creating nothing less than a new agricultural civilization. Along with traditional soil-improvement measures, Mussolini's legislation also addressed the construction of houses, the establishment of settlements, the relocation of inhabitants selected for a given project, and their professional, cultural, and political initiation into a new way of life.

The *bonifica integrale* was the Italian form of the international back-to-the-land movement, and its underlying rationale was the same there as elsewhere. After the failure of liberal capitalism, the land seemed the only solid foundation on which the nation could stand. In a sense, the reclamation of the Pontine Marshes was a settlement project expanded to the level of a whole region. Adapted along Italian lines, it included features from Ebenezer Howard's original garden city, Gottfried Feder's *Landstadt*, German geographer Walter Christaller's idea of arranging settlements around central urban nuclei, and, last but not least, the Soviet *kolchos*. As always with Fascist and National Socialist ideology, individualism and collectivism were tightly intertwined.[5] On the one hand, individuals would become small property holders whose ties to the land would assure their membership in and loyalty to the community. At the same time, collective and cooperative institutions would reinforce social cohesion. A good example of these ideas in practice were the *aziende agrarie*, communal storehouses and workshops for tractors, heavy vehicles, and other machines that would have been beyond the means of individual farmers. There was one *azienda agraria* for every hundred farms, which for social and administration purposes comprised a village, or *borgo*. The *borgo* was the basic unit of the settlement project.

A three-layered network of settlements covered the swamplands of the Agro Pontino. There were individual farms laid out in regular, almost military spatial intervals; *borghi*, which consisted of these farms and which themselves combined to form a broad-meshed network; and five newly founded cities that served as urban centers. Translated into military terms, the farms could be considered platoons, the *borghi* companies or battalions, and the cities regiments or divisions. It was as if elements of the garden city had merged with those of Roman military camps. Settlement houses bore the disproportionately large inscription "Property of the ONC" (Opera Nazionale dei Combattanti, or National Veterans Organization, which was in charge of the project) and a number. The combination of large letters and numbers made it clear that the houses were not traditional city or village residences but units organized along collective, paramilitary lines.

In contrast to other settlements of the 1930s, the settlement "camps" of the Agro Pontino were not equipped with electricity and running water—further evidence of their military inspiration. The primitive conditions are all the more puzzling because the Agro Pontino was a prestige project aimed at demonstrating the modernity of Fascism. That again raises the question of the propagandistic function of these endeavors. What was Fascism trying to say with the Agro Pontino?

WITH THEIR LACK of modern conveniences and nondescript appearance, the Agro farms were hardly an argument for the attractiveness or technological prowess of the Mussolini regime. The *borghi*, too, were merely a functional innovation with little symbolic power. As far as rural settlements were concerned, the Agro Pontino had nothing more to offer than settlement projects under the New Deal, National Socialism, or, indeed, any other system in the industrialized world, and as we have seen, the propaganda value of the American and German settlements remained scant. In fact, the farms and the *borghi* were little more than foot soldiers filling out the ranks in the propaganda campaign surrounding the Agro Pontino. Their importance was dwarfed by that of the newly founded cities: Littoria, Pontinia, Aprilia, Pomezia, and, above all, Sabaudia. (Only Littoria, Pontinia, and Sabaudia were located in the swamplands of the Agro Pontino proper. Aprilia and Pomezia were built to the northwest of that area but were considered to be part of the project in regional, civic-planning, and architectural terms.) The overall planning and staging of the Agro Pontino project was explicitly focused on these urban centers, casting them as monuments to the effort of land redemption.

Reviving an ancient Roman rite, Mussolini kicked off construction on each of the *"nuove città"* by marking the city limits with a plow. He also decreed that construction work was to take no more than a year, at which point the city would be inaugurated. At every inaugural celebration, Mussolini announced both the start and the completion dates for the next project. The spectacle gave the impression that Fascist Italy was a society that was both forever on the move and running like clockwork. The same was, of course, true for the simultaneous modernization of Italy's railroads. A short time later, with a comparable degree of pomp and speed, the construction of the German autobahn was rammed into the minds of the populace as evidence of the determination, will, and efficiency of the Nazi regime.

The static results of Mussolini's projects stood in marked contrast to the dynamism with which they were created. Once finished, his New Cities were in reality "anti-cities," though not in the sense of the garden city's urban-rural synthesis (even

Sabaudia, the "anti-city"

if Mussolini had this in mind when he coined the phrase). Instead, they became three-dimensional representations of the Fascist ideals of organization, control, and the absence of urban chaos.[6] Le Corbusier, who, in keeping with his ideological sympathies during the mid-1930s, aspired to design one of Mussolini's five cities, got it as wrong as possible when he described what was actually built as "a shepherd's idyll à la Marie Antoinette's *petit trianon*"—that is, an imitation of a simple peasant village.[7]

Instead, the *nuove città* commemorated a static order, one of permanence and immobility that offered a counterweight to the state of perpetual motion generated by and characteristic of the regime. The need for such a counterweight explains why the Fascists revived the basic layout of the Roman military camp, kept the size of the cities modest, and emphasized public buildings, especially the centrally located town halls, with their dominating towers. How little the New Cities were intended to be bustling urban centers is clear from their representation in the media. Only the pictures of the inauguration ceremonies show the streets and squares full of people; in all subsequent illustrations they are utterly deserted—much as in a military cemetery or in a painting by Giorgio de Chirico.

The comparison is anything but arbitrary since the Fascist obsession with "movement" culminated in what they considered its highest, most heroic form: battle. The Mussolini regime explicitly presented the reclamation and cultivation of the Pontine Marshes as a kind of war. At the inaugural ceremony for the city of Littoria, the tone and style of which would have been equally appropriate for the unveiling of a war memorial, Mussolini proclaimed, "What we've conquered here is a new province, and our daily labor is nothing other than a military operation in a war that we cherish above all others."[8]

Analogies to Italian soldiers' experiences in World War I were a running theme of the Agro Pontino initiative. From its very inception, the project was promoted as the fulfillment of earlier governments' promises to soldiers that they would be given a piece of land when they returned from the field of battle. That is why the national veterans' organization was put in charge of the project and why it officially owned the property concerned. The ONC coordinated and paid for land reclamation; built the houses, *borghi*, and cities; and selected the settlers. It also watched over, directed, and controlled their lives, with a discipline similar to that in a military camp.

*　　*　　*

MUSSOLINI, HOWEVER, WAS not thinking so much of the finished project when he characterized Littoria as a campaign to conquer a new province. True, the 26,000 settlers the ONC brought in from all over Italy to populate the city were well suited to symbolize the new Fascist "melting-pot" community that was to be forged in the reclaimed province, much as the nation itself had allegedly been forged during the Great War. But the real battle was the act of conquest itself, a far more dramatic event, which involved an army of workers (230,000 between 1932 and 1935), also recruited from all over the country and outnumbering the actual settlers by nearly nine to one.

In a new type of frontline reporting, the Italian media depicted their labors as a battle against nature. In his 1934 book *Terra nuova*, for instance, Corrado Alvaro raved:

> Never before has such a large territory been remade in such a short time, from one day to the next. Only in modern warfare has the like of this been seen, when two or three thousand soldiers bivouacked on a field, constructing within the space of an hour a tent city with water and sewage canals, canteens, command centers and parade grounds. . . . Both forms of invasion use similar techniques. It is thanks to modern warfare that we now know what superlatives a mass invasion can achieve.

The influx of workers "armed with pickaxes, spades, and shovels" inspired Alvaro to write of "human civilization advanc[ing] like a column of tanks." The sight of the "settlers' houses, painted blue," was "reminiscent of a well-disciplined army," and the agricultural machinery parked in the barns "could be mistaken for a new type of weaponry. . . . The earth has been ripped open like a battlefield." The arrival of new settlers prompted similar reflections:

> They assemble on the train station platform and march forth as if they are going to man the trenches. . . . [Those who are already there] ask them where they come from, and every one of them answers with raised arm, just as on the front when a battalion or a regiment marches past another.

For Italy's youth, the Agro Pontino was to take the place of World War I, which they had been too young to experience. Alvaro promoted the project as "the central point of a fundamentally new Italian way of life," adding that "today to have participated in the *bonifica* is just as significant as having taken part in war."[9]

Every year, the Agro Pontino was turned into the central "theater of war" (*teatro della guerra*), with Mussolini personally inaugurating the start of what was known as the "harvest battle" (*battaglia del grano*). One of the most iconic images of Fascism is the photo depicting a bare-chested Il Duce on a flatbed truck surrounded by harvest workers.

Battle and war as emblems of strength and creativity were just as ambiguous as the rest of the symbols and metaphors favored by Fascism. Obsessed with images of life and death, Fascism drew on the energizing and spiritualizing capacity of the interplay between the two, and the idea that a life truly worthy of heroism could not be lived without the constant presence of mortal danger. The image of arable fields conquered from swamplands by the machinery of mechanized agriculture, which had both ripped apart the soil and made it fertile, was one variation of this leitmotif. In 1932, Mussolini presided over the

Mussolini
inspiring the
troops as he
inaugurates the
wheat harvest
in the Pontine
Marshes

inaugural ceremony of Littoria in the style of a military field
commander, with 110 advancing tractors and trucks forming a
broad front line. The event was described with heroic pathos:

> The gaze of the Duce, deeply satisfied, rests upon the
> majestic gathering of machines created by man in order
> to redeem the earth; the vision that glimmers forth in
> the Chief's eyes: that of the imperial destiny of Rome
> resuscitated through the furrows' fertilizing powers.

This author also wrote of the plow's dual "wounding and fertil-izing action."[10]

Such images of land being reclaimed from swamp also called up biblical associations, specifically of the creation of earth from the waters in Genesis. Yet biblical imagery—precisely because it, unlike the martial and sexual symbolism otherwise promoted by the Fascists, was already well established in the nation's collective mind—had to be subjected to a particularly violent reclamation by Mussolini's propaganda. Fascist accounts of "battle against" and "victory over" the water (*lotta con l'acqua, conquista sull'acqua*) were not only secularized retellings of Gen-esis, a triumph of technological struggle in which a natural ele-ment had been subjugated and conquered; they also symbolized Fascism's political battle. For ultimately the true enemy was not water but the mud of the swamplands, that murky slime which for the modern psyche has perennially called to mind bottomless chaos, the threat of the feminine lack of order, and anarchic impurity. The separation of undefined morass into *pure* elements—in this case, earth and water—has from time immemorial been the goal of all attempts to create order, and in the Fascist imagination, Mussolini's rise to power in 1922 had reclaimed the nation from the "swamp" of the liberal par-liamentary system. A popular 1935 open-air spectacle made an explicit—and highly derogatory—reference to Italy's parliamen-tarian past: "Off in a hollow to the left of the stage a swamp comes into view. . . . Filled with reeds and bubbling with mud, it emanates steam and froglike croakings intermingled with voices of rumor, calumny, and doubt."[11] The true significance of the Agro Pontino for Mussolini and his regime was as an epic tale, a mixture of reality and symbolism, in which they could reenact the earlier political struggle of their rise to power.

A comparison between the Agro Pontino and the great public works projects of National Socialism and the New Deal—the autobahn and the Tennessee Valley Authority—reveals a common striving for technological monumentalism that would modernize and re-form entire landscapes or, to use the terminology of the 1930s, regions. Without doubt, the Agro Pontino represented a major achievement in drainage, construction, and agricultural technology. Yet it also ultimately differed from the TVA dams, the autobahn, and the Dnieper power plants—all projects in which the monumentalism resided in the technology itself. The Agro Pontino was more like a settlement, albeit one whose scope overshadowed all previous projects and whose New Cities certainly provided monumentality. It did not measure up, in either technical scale or dynamism, to the projects simultaneously undertaken in the United States and in Germany.[12]

The Tennessee Valley Authority

In May 1933, President Roosevelt signed the Tennessee Valley Authority Act, which authorized the federal government to take over the regional development of parts of Tennessee, Alabama, Georgia, Mississippi, North Carolina, Kentucky, and Virginia. The region, which surrounded the Tennessee River and its tributaries, was some 39,000 square miles in area, or 125 times as large as the Pontine Marshes. It was one of the poorest regions in America. Median per capita income among its 2.5 million inhabitants was less than half of the national average, even though the area had originally been blessed with resources that should have made it prosperous, including fertile land, a mild climate, and sufficient rainfall. Two generations earlier, the Tennessee Valley had seemed predestined to become a kind of California. But then, at the end of the nineteenth century, came robber-baron capitalism, and the region suffered dramatically. Within the space of a few years, its forests were felled, leading to massive soil erosion and turning broad stretches of fertile farmland into a lunar landscape.

Sixteen years before the TVA act, Washington had already initiated a major construction project in the area: the Wilson Dam, near Muscle Shoals, Alabama. The dam, constructed in 1917 and 1918 as part of the state-directed wartime economy, was intended to provide the energy necessary to power the nearby munitions industry. But it never went operational. The end of the war and of state intervention in the economy soon turned the facility into a costly ruin. Privatization was not an option since the utility corporations that would have been the likely candidates to take over the dam were rocked by scandals during the 1920s and thus discredited in public opinion.

The project seemed to have found an investor of an entirely different caliber in 1921, when Henry Ford offered $5 million in return for a century-long lease on the facility. His development concept prefigured the initiatives later undertaken by the TVA, encompassing the construction of additional dams and a vision for remaking the whole area that married the two ideals of motorization and electrification. Ford planned to erect a mixed industrial and agricultural strip city along the lines of Ebenezer

Woman on the porch of a drought-stricken farmstead near the Smoky Mountains, February 1939

Howard's ideas, which would have run seventy-five miles long and fifteen miles wide along the Tennessee River. The prospective community, its inhabitants "saturated" with power and cars, was to be a model for the future, extending Ford's system of production and consumption from the automobile industry—the same community makes and buys the cars—to energy. This vision played well to the public because it promised to merge the two most modern forms of technology, personified by Henry Ford and Thomas Edison, who made a joint public appearance in Muscle Shoals in 1922 as codirectors of the enterprise. Another source of appeal was the plan's manifest populist élan. Just as he had built his automobile empire without the help of banks—indeed, in opposition to Wall Street—Ford now pledged to lead the Muscle Shoals project in the interests of consumers—the people—and to strike a blow against finance capitalists and energy corporations. But Ford's plan went nowhere, thanks in large measure to senator George Norris, who mistrusted Ford's intentions and thought the project should remain in public hands. Ford withdrew his offer in 1924.[13]

THE GROUNDWORK HAD thus been well laid when Roosevelt trained his sights on the Tennessee Valley as a target for regional development. Like the Agro Pontino, the area had become a symbol whose national importance far exceeded its actual regional significance.[14] And just as the reclamation of the Pontine Marshes became the showpiece of the *bonifica integrale*, the TVA became the great emblem of the New Deal's aspirations toward integrated regional development. The TVA did not restrict itself to a single sector—settlement construction, transportation, agriculture, or industry—but coordinated all of them into a coherent strategy.

While the reclamation of the Agro Pontino, despite its New Cities, remained essentially an agricultural project, the TVA aimed at a new type of synthesis between agriculture and technology. On the surface, the TVA seemed to separate the two into discrete, unrelated enterprises. One focused on water: the construction of dams and sluices was intended to prevent flooding and make the rivers navigable. The other focused on land: forestation and soil improvement were to restore the land to its original condition before the overexploitation of the late nineteenth century, while infrastructural improvements would transform the area into an exemplary modern region. These two spheres of activity were connected insofar as the damming of rivers flooded whole valleys, necessitating the resettlement of all those who lived there. Conservative critics saw this as driving the farmers from their land, but New Deal propaganda boasted of the new world that would arise to replace the one that had been submerged. This new world was to be neither a re-creation of the old one a few hundred yards above the newly elevated water levels nor, as was the case with the Agro Pontino, an agricultural community with a few symbols of modernization. What made the TVA project different was the central role played by electricity.

Along with the goal of integrated development, another element shared by both the American and the Italian projects was their presentation as national endeavors, comparable to both countries' efforts in World War I. Roosevelt's rhetorical comparisons between the fight against the Depression and war against an external enemy encouraged a vision of the TVA as the extension of the activities begun in Muscle Shoals in 1917. The way the TVA was organized also called to mind the Great War. The TVA was a "public corporation"—a state-owned legal and economic entity established to perform a specific non-state and non-military task under government control. The hybrid structure had been created in Washington in 1917 to allow the government to better direct the arms industry and to initiate supporting projects such as the Wilson Dam. The public corporation was the federal government's way around a legal system and a constitution that prohibited the state from engaging in economic entrepreneurship. That did nothing, of course, to obscure the fact that the TVA was, as Roosevelt himself defined it, "a corporation clothed with the power of Government but possessed of the flexibility and initiative of a private enterprise." There was considerable concern at the time as to whether the president was subverting the U.S. Constitution. Political scientist David Mitrany wrote:

> The TVA has really introduced *a new dimension into the constitutional structure* of the United States—*without any formal change in the Constitution.* Acting as an autonomous authority, it has entered into contractual relations with the individual States of the region, their institutions and local sub-divisions; these relations have grown together into a co-operative, unified, multi-purpose undertaking which crosses and envelops all political boundary lines. That was practicable because the TVA's jurisdiction was limited to the functions entrusted to it by Congress—another case of *full powers for a limited function* [emphasis added].

In other words, the TVA posed every bit as great a challenge to the liberal-democratic principle of separation of powers as Roosevelt's plebiscitary-charismatic leadership style itself. The main difference as compared with the ONC's role in the Agro Pontino was that the TVA did not own the entire region under its authority but only the Tennessee River and its tributaries, together with the dams and power stations the government built there. Yet insofar as the rivers made up the natural infrastructure of the region, the state effectively controlled the entire area.[15]

THIS IS PERHAPS an appropriate point to take a closer look at the natural element that was the focus—one could almost say the enemy—of both the TVA and the Agro Pontino initiatives, as well as their model, the Dnieper dam in the Soviet Union. Water was both reality and symbol. The real results to be achieved by the three projects—the draining of a swamp and the regulation of two raging rivers—were clear enough, and as we have seen, for the Fascist mind, the Pontine Marshes symbolized the ineffectual nattering of the Italian bourgeoisie, who had been unable to modernize the nation. But what did the taming of the wild waters of the Tennessee River signify for Americans?

A description of the Tennessee Valley ten years after the start of Roosevelt's project gives us an insight into its meaning and symbolic importance:

> This is the story of a great change. It is a tale of a wandering and inconstant river now become a chain of broad and lovely lakes which people enjoy, and on which they can depend, in all seasons, for the movement of barges of commerce that now nourish their business enterprises. It is a story of how waters once wasted and destructive have been controlled and now work, night and day, creating electric energy to lighten the burden of human drudgery. Here is a tale of fields grown old and barren with the years, which now are vigorous with new fertility, lying green to the sun; of forests that were hacked and despoiled, now protected and refreshed with strong young trees.[16]

Thus David Lilienthal, a member of the TVA's first board of directors, began his 1944 book on the early years of the project, entitled *TVA: Democracy on the March*. There is hardly a better source for comprehending the TVA's symbolic dimension within the New Deal. Lilienthal does not describe just the technical aspects of the regulation of the Tennessee River and its tributaries; his words suggest an analogy, probably unconscious, with the New Deal's successful regulation of liberal capitalism. His account of how the TVA's dams and sluices put an end to the catastrophic floods of the past calls to mind the image of rampant capitalism being reined in and productively channeled by Keynesian economic planning. What the New Deal achieved in the Tennessee Valley with dams it brought about economically through numerous regulatory agencies. The TVA was the concrete-and-steel realization of the regulatory authority at the heart of the New Deal. In this sense, the massive dams in the Tennessee Valley were monuments to the New Deal, just as the New Cities in the Pontine Marshes were monuments to Fascism.

The TVA was particularly valuable as a propaganda asset because the idea of technological regulation and planning was accepted, even welcomed by a society which otherwise rejected all forms of political or economic control. Technical facilities for controlling floods were like a Trojan horse in the belly of which economic and social planning could be smuggled into the liberal-capitalist bastion of America. One of Lilienthal's colleagues on the TVA board of directors, Arthur E. Morgan, wrote in 1934:

> We are beginning with a design of a water-control system, with flood-control, with forestry, balancing agriculture and industry, prevention of land exploitation, and vocational reorganization. Any one of these jobs takes us into all the others. We find ourselves thus working out a philosophy of social organization.[17]

The architecture of power: the concrete mass of the Norris Dam

Morgan was later described as "both a civil engineer and a social engineer" who believed that technological and social planning were parallel evolutionary phenomena. Even liberals, for whom totalitarianism was the great enemy, unquestioningly accepted the technological, economic, and social "totality" of the TVA. One such liberal, Julian Huxley, went so far as to characterize it as evidence that "planning cannot only be reconciled with individual freedom and opportunity, but can be used to enhance and enlarge them."[18]

THE TVA HAD the political, symbolic, and rhetorical task of demonstrating democracy's ability to compete with and, indeed, surpass totalitarianism's achievements in the realm of planning. But beyond that, TVA propaganda was also directed against an internal enemy: the capitalist excesses that had led to the Depression and that were perceived to pose as great a threat to democracy as Hitler, Stalin, or Mussolini. This enemy was personified not only by "Wall Street"—the financial demon which according to the popular imagination had perverted the benevolent, democratic principle of money—but also by the electric power industry. The large utility companies, many people believed, kept the nation's most important source of energy in a virtual stranglehold, much as the banks had maintained cutthroat control over its capital resources.

America had the reputation of being the most advanced nation on earth as far as electrification was concerned. Le Corbusier waxed poetic about the "electric Milky Way" of the nighttime Manhattan skyline, and American electrical appliances elicited envy the world over. But that was only one side of the story. Major urban centers were the only parts of America that were fully electrified. The countryside was kept literally in the dark because there was no profit to be made in rural power. In 1930, only 20 percent of American households had access to electricity. Capitalism, so it seemed, had let down, even betrayed, consumers. This shortcoming appeared all the less pardonable in the wake of Ford's mass production of automobiles, which had shown that technological innovation could make basic conveniences affordable to the population at large. Ford's adversary over the Wilson Dam, Senator George Norris, a progressive Republican in the style of Teddy Roosevelt, laid the blame squarely at the feet of the utility companies:

The power trust is the greatest monopolistic corporation that has been organized for private greed. . . . It has
bought and sold legislatures. . . . It has managed to infest
farm organization; it has not hesitated to enter the
sacred walls of churches and religious organizations. . . .
With its slimy fingers it reaches into every community
and levies its tribute upon every fireside. There is not an
avenue of human activity that it has not undertaken to
control. It has undertaken to poison the minds of our
boys in the Boy Scout organization. It has undertaken to
bribe the minister in the pulpit, and with its sinister
stealthy tread, it has even entered our public schools and
tried to poison the minds of the children.[19]

Popular anger at the electricity monopolies was new, and for
that reason more intense than people's centuries-old hostility
toward banks. Whereas banks had never elicited broad enthusiasm, the idea of electrification had, since entering the realm
of possibility around 1900, raised immense public expectations.
Much as technology in general figured in utopian visions of the
future, electrification was seen to hold the promise of salvation
from drudgery and exploitation. In his 1901 novel *Work*,
French author Émile Zola gives us one version of this paradise
on earth:

The machines did everything. . . . What an elevating
sight: an army of obedient mechanical laborers with never-
tiring stamina . . . that were now the worker's friends,
instead of their competitors. . . . They liberated instead
of exploiting him. While he rested, they did his work.[20]

At the time Zola's vision was read not as the product of an over-
heated literary imagination, but as an expression of what could

be called the electric spirit of the age. If we compare Zola's utopia with Norris's "J'accuse," we can see just how wide a gap had opened between people's expectations of salvation and their reality.

Electricity was considered the purest and most efficient form of energy, in comparison to which all previous advances in technology and industry appeared primitive. What Lewis Mumford called the "paleo-technology" of the steam engine had driven the first industrial revolution; now electricity had arrived to bring the second industrial revolution to its "neo-technological" conclusion. Electric power was credited with the potential "to redeem all the dreams betrayed by the machine" and to create "an industrial Eden."[21] This was a belief shared by such diverse characters as Charles Steinmetz, chief engineer for General Electric, and Vladimir Lenin, founder of the Soviet Union.

LIKE CHARISMATIC LEADERSHIP, nationalism, and regionalism, electrification was an earlier idea that enjoyed a renaissance in the 1930s. As with the other key ideas, the main difference between the Roosevelt-era version of electrification and its earlier expression at the turn of the century was that the vision no longer issued from a society bursting with vitality and wealth, but from the experience of decline and collapse. Electrification was no longer lionized as the latest technological advance that would realize a marvelous industrial civilization of ever-increasing, miraculously hygienic, drudgery-free productivity. Instead, it was seen as a means of retreat from what was perceived as the great historical error of industrialization.

Just as the region was held up as an "organic" space, and the autarkic settlement as a firmly anchored, crisis-resistant social and economic unit, electricity was now considered the only technology that could liberate humanity from the prison of large-scale industry and restore the decent conditions of the past.

The central concept was decentralization: a reversal of the previous trend toward industrial concentration in favor of a Rousseauian mixed economy of agriculture and light industry, in which human beings would no longer feel like appendages to some distant, anonymous command center but would reclaim control over their lives. Electrification was the technological means of regaining the advantages of premodern society—craftsmanship, communal solidarity, and authenticity—without having to return to a primitive standard of living. Decentralized and miniaturized into individual household appliances and small-scale motors, electricity would create the first industrial civilization in which people would act as both sovereign producer and consumer.

The obvious objection to this perspective was that since energy was still produced by large plants, such decentralization was purely illusory; but that criticism held no weight among electrification advocates. The electricity produced by the TVA was, in their eyes, power made by and for the people, much as the Volkswagen in Germany was, as its name proclaimed, a "people's car." Whereas the opposition between big and small in the liberal system had always entailed the threat to the latter of being subjugated and devoured by the former, Fascism, National Socialism, and the New Deal skirted the issue by maintaining that large industrial conglomerations, once under state control, were nothing but the convergence and collective property of many small consumers and owners. "Big" had a responsibility to protect "small" and guarantee its survival. Or as Walter Creese, a leading expert on the period put it, "'Big' was intended to have 'little' implications around it. The huge concrete dams were supposed to cause the countryside to become more habitable, symbiotic, prosperous, bucolic and receptive."

Creese, the author of the most enlightening study of the TVA's cultural and mythological import, cites the model settlement of Norristown, located in the shadow of the Norris Dam, as an example of such protectionism. Norristown resembled a charming eighteenth-century village, with quaint "doll houses" set off against the background of the dam's monumental concrete wall, which can almost be seen as safeguarding the community much in the fashion of a medieval town wall.[22] A similar juxtaposition existed in the Agro Pontino, where humble settlements were both overshadowed and sheltered by the monumental party and government buildings of the New Cities. But while Mussolini's project was more Roman Empire than twentieth century in its architectural, technical, and sociological orientation, Roosevelt's TVA featured state-of-the-art construction, energy technology, social theories and propaganda needs. Lewis Mumford, the man who coined the phrase "architecture of power," pronounced the TVA dams a successful marriage of technological and political power. He could equally well have paraphrased Lenin and said that the New Deal plus electrification equaled the welfare state, or joined with another contemporary critic who spoke of an "architecture of public relations."[23] A more symbolically potent construction project is hard to imagine. The dam represented a taming and civilizing power that transformed the destructive natural force of water into usable energy. It also created a kind of economic protectorate, outside the reach of big business, controlled by the people via their elected representatives. It is no wonder, then, that the dam became the central emblem of the New Deal.

There were many contemporary comparisons with the pyramids of ancient Egypt, medieval cathedrals, the Acropolis, and the Forum Romanum. But the aims of the TVA were more original and innovative than mere reproduction of historical grandeur. From the very inception of the project, the planners and builders strove to link architectural and technological efficiency with the suggestive power of propaganda. In his opening address for a 1941 exhibit at the Museum of Modern Art on the architecture of the TVA, David Lilienthal proclaimed, "Millions of Americans . . . will see these structures. They will see in them a kind of a token of the virility and vigor of democracy. When people see these dams that they own and were built for them, we want their hearts to be moved with pride."[24]

By "millions" Lilienthal meant the masses who would see images of the dams in various forms of media, from independent journalism to government propaganda. *Life* magazine, which was itself founded in the 1930s, was an essential conduit of the New Deal's and, especially, the TVA's public iconography. Such reports were, as we have seen, thoroughly informed by public relations handouts from Washington. The level of influence reached new heights with "newsreels" about the TVA commissioned by Washington and provided to schools and theaters free of charge. As one recent historian points out, "little effort was made to inform the audiences that such films were not fact-based newsreels."[25]

But Lilienthal was also referring to firsthand experience. The TVA dams were conceived not just as power-producing facilities but also as attractions for streams of tourists, who, like pilgrims at a shrine, were to visit the installations and so take symbolic possession of them. Amenities such as access roads, visitors' centers, reception halls, observation platforms, and spectators' galleries were part of the facilities' overall design. These were so well integrated that it was difficult to distinguish where technology ended and propaganda began. This blurring of the lines necessitated careful organization to keep the stream of tourists from disrupting operational activities. Historian Talbot Hamlin described one such tourist visit as follows:

> The public flowed into the structure on the ground level, went through the display room and the visitors' office, then along the upper galleries looking down into the powerhouse, and so out again, without ever crossing any line of ordinary working traffic. They are shown everything without interfering with any worker, and this alone entailed the most careful circulation planning.[26]

The spatial impression made on visitors by one of the dam facilities' reception halls was compared to the awe inspired by the lobbies of the era's palatial movie theaters.[27]

Even the purely technical areas were framed in monumental fashion so as to maximize impact. The generator room at one of the dams, for instance, reminded a contemporary architecture critic of the interior of a temple. Space and energy were combined in a spectacle whose effect on visitors was eerily analogous to that of the Nuremberg rallies staged by Albert Speer, with their dramatic "Cathedral of Light" effects. "You sense the powerful operations of the dynamos," one journalist wrote of the dams in 1940.

> It is an hypnotic experience. Your ears are filled with the insistent hum of the powerful generators, your eyes are filled with the impression of strong mechanical and structural forms. The total impression is complete, everything contributes to the one major effect. You are in the presence of the most impressive symbol of ultimate force the age has produced.[28]

And, one might add, the most impressive expression of the technical sublime. It was impossible here not to be awed by the power of the state that had created such a wonder.

The Autobahn

The emphasis on cutting-edge technology is a feature common to both the German and the American public works projects, and one that distinguishes them from Mussolini's undertaking in Italy. Motorization was for the autobahn what electrification was for the TVA: a promise that, ever since its emergence around the turn of the century, had implied not just increased convenience but also a kind of symbolic salvation. Both endeavors marked the end of the "primitive," production-oriented first phase of the industrial revolution and opened up the prospect of a consumer's paradise. In the fantasies they occasioned, all clashes between mankind and nature, technology and energy would be resolved in a neo-Saint-Simonian synthesis. Aside from a brief interruption during World War I, the twentieth-century imagination was utterly captivated by the idea of mass access to cars and electricity, and that fascination increased in 1933, when the state took on a more active role in daily life. Roosevelt and Hitler, who staked their political fortunes on the TVA and the autobahn respectively, were only too aware of the powerful public desires these projects harnessed on behalf of their governments.

The reason the Third Reich focused on motorization and not electrification was simple. By 1930 most German households, even in rural areas, already had electrical power, but few people owned an automobile. Just as individualistic liberalism in the United States had led to the rise of the automotive industry, the corporative-communal organization of energy production in Germany had succeeded in electrifying the countryside. The two societies were thus mirror images of each other: in America, many car owners lacked power in their homes, while in Germany, people who could plug appliances into wall sockets were dependent on public or nonmotorized transportation. In both countries, the state intervened as the only authority capable of balancing the deficit. Both Hitler and Roosevelt owed a great deal of their charisma to their ability to neutralize the special interests, nationalize industry, and provide the masses with access to "miracle" technologies.

AS IS THE case with all novel products, from revolution to fashion, new technologies possess their greatest appeal in the early days, when they are first introduced. The prospect that an evolving technology might fulfill age-old human dreams calls forth boundless awe and admiration. Later, once a technology enters the phase of mass production and mass consumption, that effect wears off.

By the end of the 1920s in America, the automobile had ceased to represent a miracle of technology, but in Europe— and especially in Germany and Italy—the auto retained its futuristic appeal. Cars were mobility- and speed-generating machines that allowed people to exceed their natural limits and technologically magnify their power. Europeans used cars as weapons to secure and safeguard their personal freedom, and European driving styles, it was noted, were correspondingly individualistic: aggressive, breakneck, and inconsiderate. Europeans visiting the United States were surprised at how calm, conformist, and passive American drivers were. This, as some realized, was due simply to the sheer number of cars and the amount of traffic. Nonetheless, one French observer even interpreted American patience on the roads as an extension of political conformism or, as he praised it, a "remarkable aptitude for a certain social discipline,"[29] also expressed in the stability of American democracy.

Historians of the Third Reich originally treated the autobahn as a subsidiary endeavor within the Nazis' rearmament of Germany. The network of highways, they concluded, was strategically planned to serve a regime that was, from its earliest days in power, bent on war. In the past thirty years, as approaches to National Socialism have become more differentiated, a multidimensional picture of the autobahn project has emerged. The autobahn is now seen as the primary example of the other, "American" side of the Nazi regime, which applied manipulation and persuasion, rather than coercion, to elicit public loyalty. The ideology of "the people's community," or

Volksgemeinschaft, a new generation of historians discovered, was successful not because it promised bread and circuses but because it delivered them. From this vantage point, the Third Reich seems less a prison than a gigantic recreational park, run by organizations like the Strength Through Joy holiday-allocation program and held together by the autobahn.

To make any sense, Strength Through Joy and the autobahn required a third major project: the Volkswagen. The idea for a people's car that could carry five passengers, cruise at speeds of up to sixty miles per hour, and cost only 1,000 reichsmarks was the product of a meeting in 1933 between Adolf Hitler and automobile designer Ferdinand Porsche. After many delays, construction on the car began in 1938 under the auspices of the Strength Through Joy program. In fact, the precursor to the VW Beetle was known as the "Strength Through Joy car."

Construction on the autobahn, the world's first limited access road network, had begun five years earlier, shortly after the Nazis took power in 1933, and the first section was completed by 1935. The surprising fact that roads were built before there were cars to drive on them did nothing to decrease the psychological impact of the project. Just the opposite. Unlike in America, where the rapid spread of cars had made motoring a routine activity, the autobahn and its promise of mass motorization only enhanced the charisma of the automobile. It was like the torso of an antique sculpture, whose missing parts the viewer was required to fill in for himself. The imagined results were such as could hardly have been matched by the completed highway system filled with cars.

*   *   *

THE CONCRETE SURFACES of the autobahn were another example of the "architecture of power"—in the sense of both technological and governmental achievement. There was also an association with the idea of energy, since the German terms for both "motor vehicle" and "motorway," *Kraftfahrzeug* and *Kraftfahrbahn*, contain the word *Kraft*, which literally means power. "Hitler's roads," as the highways were called, could thus be seen as the concrete equivalent of a national power grid, a new type of monumentalism whose national scope dwarfed that of regional projects like the Agro Pontino, and even the TVA.

All these public works had the same purpose: to regenerate and modernize the nation, which was perceived to have been ruined by liberalsim—physically as well as economically. But while the Argo Pontino and the TVA attempted to do this by showcasing technological and economic modernization, the autobahn also focused on aesthetics. In the end, of course, all three projects depended on the mass media to produce the intended effect. As the majority of Americans, Italians, and Germans either lived too far away from the promised lands of the Agro Pontino and the TVA, or did not own a car for traveling on the autobahn, they relied on newsreels, illustrated magazines, broadsheets, and exhibitions to experience these great construction sites of modernity. But what was the deeper meaning of the autobahn? What was it intended to convey to the nation?

There was a certain inconsistency, if not ambivalence, even in the term *autobahn*. Containing the word *Bahn* (as in *Eisenbahn*: railway), it suggested that something qualitatively different from a traditional road was intended. The ambivalence was enhanced by the fact that the state railway administration was commissioned to oversee the planning and directing of the autobahn construction, but in reality it had limited control. The situation prepared the ground for an ongoing conflict among the various factions involved. While some saw the *Eisenbahn* as the model for the network of highways, others wanted to create an entirely new aesthetic of space and movement. Hitler's personally appointed autobahn supervisor, Fritz Todt, and a special handpicked advisory committee of landscape architects considered Germany's rail system a model better ignored. Their guiding ideal was a vision of "German technology," an almost mystical phrase that carried a double promise: to free technology from capitalism's "enslavement" and then reconcile it with nature.[30] To these planners, the railway had been the main destroyer of the "organic" landscape; now the autobahn was to serve as its main redeemer.

In one of his central statements, Todt tried to specify what this meant for the construction of the autobahn:

> The question of landscape design is one of the most important for the autobahn. . . . I'm very concerned that the various routes, when they are developed, do not give the impression of being artificial stretches, as is the case with railroad tracks. On the contrary, people should feel that they are being connected with nature.

The autobahn, Todt added, "should be a tightly drawn, indestructible band connecting technology and nature." Other planners intended "not to destroy the scenery but to emphasize the particular character of each individual landscape through the sensitivity with which [the autobahn's] routes are laid out." The ulti-

The autobahn as the apotheosis of nature

mate goal was "not the shortest but, rather, the most sublime connection between two points," designed to "make the landscape more beautiful than it was before."[31]

THE QUESTION AS to whether these lofty goals were simply propaganda or whether the autobahn represented a genuine ecological achievement of Nazism continues to occupy historians today. With the demise of the military-strategic thesis in the 1980s, scholars swung around to the other extreme and began to "overinterpret"[32] Hitler's highways as a conservationist endeavor. Historian Thomas Zeller has recently accused this school of taking Nazi rhetoric at face value, pointing out that as a rule engineers, not environmentalists, determined the routes the autobahn followed. But instead of pursuing the perennial discrepancies between intentions and reality, perhaps we would be better off asking what these planners actually meant by the "particular character" of the landscape, the "band connecting technology and nature," and the "sublime connection."

From the very inception of the autobahn project, such phrases gave rise to misunderstandings. A number of the landscape architects on Todt's advisory committee assumed he meant that the autobahn should be laid out so as to preserve the landscape through which it ran. They soon found out, however, that what he had in mind was not landscape preservation but "landscape creation."[33] Those who protested, for instance, against plans to build the autobahn through the Siebengebirge conservation area near Bonn were quickly dismissed as "fainthearted nature lovers." The Siebengebirge autobahn was built as planned, with Todt arguing that the highway not only made the beauty of the area accessible but actually represented an aesthetic improvement on it.[34]

Todt also characterized the autobahn as the "crown of the surrounding landscape." It is not clear whether he was playing on Weimar-era Expressionist architect Bruno Taut's famous idea of the "city crown"—the sparking visual focus of the city. But numerous commentators have drawn comparisons between

Expressionist and National Socialist visions of naturalized technology and technologized nature, setting Todt's autobahn-landscape next to Taut's city crown as well as to his vision of an "Alpine architecture that would grow organically like a crystal from mountain cliffs."[35]

To understand the intended aesthetics of the autobahn, it is perhaps best to look to the type of American road that—more so, for instance, than the *autostrada* in Fascist Italy—served German planners as a model.[36] In conjunction with the country's first automotive boom in the years before World War I, American planners built a series of parkways: four-lane roads that were free of crossings, separate from the ordinary street network, and reserved for passenger cars. They were "pleasure roads" that, like the autobahn, followed not the shortest but the most scenic routes. They were built for recreational driving or, as it was later known in 1930s Germany, "automotive hiking." Planners did not try to avoid curves or steep rises or drops. On the contrary, the road followed the three-dimensional contours of the landscape, merging, in novel and pleasurable fashion, the experience of driving and of enjoying nature. Describing his parkway experience in 1941 Sigfried Giedion wrote, "Freedom was given to both driver and car. Riding up and down the long sweeping grades produced an exhilarating dual feeling, one of being connected with the soil and yet of hovering just above it, a feeling like nothing else so much as sliding swiftly on skis through untouched snow down the sides of high mountains."[37]

The parkways' function was to make driving fun. They did not aim to serve as an architectural fulfillment, or crown, of the surrounding landscape. This was true of both the earliest local parkways as well as the national, tourist-oriented ones built under the New Deal. Of the latter, the 480-mile-long Blue Ridge Parkway, which began and ended in TVA territory, is the most famous example. The Blue Ridge Parkway was a model of how to make a road almost disappear from the scenery. With its two extremely narrow lanes, it resembled a paved wagon trail more than an automotive street. Instead of crowning the landscape, the road did its best to hide itself from view.

IT WAS NATURAL for a regime that had decided to pursue mass motorization as a means of social engineering to be interested in parkways. It was also inevitable that the American model would be adapted to fit the specific needs of National Socialist Germany. The most significant difference was that rather than innocuously blending into the landscape, the autobahn was intended to stand out as a conspicuous structural landmark and monument: the crowning achievement that restored the landscape to its former pristine state while bringing it up to date with the technological age. The autobahn was allowed to unfold in all its massive size and scope. Its curves were not discreetly hidden—on the contrary, they represented a dance performed in concrete. The point of "the sweeping highway,"[38] as the autobahn was called, was to instill both the landscape and the people who drove through it with a historically unprecedented dynamic force, like that which the Third Reich claimed for itself.

Regime propagandists were the most rhapsodic in celebrating this infusion of positive energy, but they were not alone in singing the praises of the autobahn. Nazi chief press spokesman

Wilfrid Bade declared: "A great calm hangs over the führer's roads. With grandeur and simplicity, they become part of the landscape . . . in the same way, they invite the driver into a blissful union with nature, which in turn embraces him like a mother welcoming home a long-lost son."

Heinrich Hauser, a non-Nazi conservative author who later emigrated to the United States, was hardly less effusive: "After a couple of minutes, we are overcome by an unbelievably delightful feeling of security, a sense of sweeping along free of gravity, very similar to the experience of flying."

Walter Dirks, a Catholic liberal and an opponent of the Hitler regime, struck much the same tone in a 1938 newspaper article for the *Frankfurter Zeitung*:

> It's not the sort of street upon which you drive with hectic activity, passing by this or that tree or house, avoiding this or that obstacle, braking, accelerating, shifting gears, depressing the clutch, and honking your horn. On a normal road, we're the ones doing the driving—the motor is just the thing that provides the power. On the autobahn we no longer seem to be doing much of anything at all. In scarcely noticeable fashion, almost unconsciously, we operate and steer the car, which we have pointed in a certain direction but which now seems to roll along the strip of the highway without any participation on our part. Even the phrase "rolling along" seems misplaced since it's hard to imagine wheels rolling under us. The car seems to be gliding. It is a mark of how passive we are, of how much the sweep of the road affects our senses, that the relationship between driver and road seems to be reversed. The road takes the active role, moving toward us quickly and smoothly, without resistance or friction, sucking the car inexorably into itself.[39]

If we compare Dirks's description of the autobahn with Giedion's account of the parkways, we see that a nearly identical driving experience, physically and technologically, could prompt diametrically opposed psychological sensations. Driving on the parkway apparently increased drivers' sense of individual power and freedom, whereas the autobahn had the uncanny effect of inducing an almost drug-like state of passivity. It is tempting to conclude that the parkway fostered a liberal-individualist mentality and the autobahn a totalitarian one. Thus one historian's pop-analytical interpetation of autobahn-reveries like Walter Dirks's and Wilfrid Bade's as "the fantasy of the Ego symbiotically dissolving into the mother-child dyad."[40]

"The car seems to be gliding. . . . The road takes the active role, moving toward us quickly and smoothly, without resistance or friction, sucking the car inexorably into itself."

This raises the question of whether someone like Bade would have also experienced the American parkway as a triumph of personal freedom, or whether that feeling was a projection of Sigfried Giedion's own liberalism. Perhaps Walter Dirks, had he traveled to America, would have felt the same way about the parkway as he did about the autobahn. Numerous examples from the literature on the autobahn show how much individual taste, temperament, and, above all, political orientation influenced people's perceptions. In a book highly critical of the Third Reich, *The House That Hitler Built*, 1930s British historian Stephen Henry Roberts characterized the autobahn as the epitome of the Third Reich:

> These straight white roads are very typical of Nazi Germany. They are needlessly grandiose but most impressive. Efficiently made and more efficiently managed, they somehow reduce the individual to insignificance. One comes to cease thinking and to realize that one is only an automaton in a machine age. They are boring, mechanical, and rather inhuman; and after a time, one feels like making a stand for individualism by zigzagging hither and thither instead of keeping in place on the straight white lines.[41]

Placed next to Roberts's one-dimensional polemic, Dirks's description of the autobahn emerges in all its ambiguity. Reading between the lines, Dirks's audience may have found in his seemingly non-commital article a more subtle criticism of totalitarian uniformity and passivity, than that hammered home by the visiting British historian. That, of course, is impossible to prove, but it is suggestive that the paper for which Dirks wrote, the *Frankfurter Zeitung*, prior to being shut down in 1943, was the leading organ in Germany for Aesopian criticism of the Hitler regime.

The title of Dirks's article was "The Triangle on the Autobahn," which referred to the route from Frankfurt to Berlin to Munich and back to Frankfurt that Dirks had driven. But for readers who remembered the language of the Weimar-era New Objectivity movement,[42] the word "triangle" had a special resonance. The triangular railroad crossing in Berlin, the *Gleisdreieck*, was a well-known site that had come to symbolize the omnipresence and omnipotence—that is, the totalitarian potential—of modern technology. One of the most famous paeans to modern technology over and against antiquated humanity was Joseph Roth's "Affirmation of the Triangular Railway Junction." Roth was associated with the New Objectivity movement, and his essay appeared in 1924, also in the *Frankfurter Zeitung*. He wrote:

> In the triangles of tracks, the great, shining iron rails flow into one another, draw electricity and take on energy for their long journeys into the world beyond. . . . They are stronger than the weakling who despises them and is afraid of them. They will not merely outlast him: They will crush him. . . . The durability of iron, a material that isn't subject to fatigue, is the highest form of life, livingness struck from unyielding, equable, steady material. What holds sway in the arena of my triangular railroad junction is the decision of the logical brain, which, to be sure of success, has implanted itself in a body of unconditional certainty: in the body of a machine. . . . That's why everything human in this

metal arena is small and feeble and lost, reduced to an insignificant supporting role in the grand enterprise. . . . Can little heartbeats still make themselves heard where a big booming one deafens a world? . . . The world to come will be like this triangular railroad junction, raised to some unknown power.[43]

EPILOGUE:
"AS WE GO MARCHING"

One year before the end of World War II, American isolationist John T. Flynn published a book entitled *As We Go Marching*, which summarized all his criticisms of the New Deal. Flynn has fallen into almost total obscurity—the perennial fate of history's losers, whose prognostications for the future are left to wait until historical developments make them once again seem relevant and they are rediscovered by a new generation. The entire intellectual content of so-called American isolationism in the 1930s has fallen into such obscurity, just as in Germany no one remembers the antinationalist opponents of Bismarck and the Wilhelmine empire. After Pearl Harbor, opposition to America's participation in World War II was considered tantamount to treason.

Along with respected intellectuals like Daniel Burnham, Alfred Bingham, and Lawrence Dennis, who was unfairly pilloried as a Fascist sympathizer, Flynn was one of the most insightful analysts of the New Deal. While none of these men equated the Roosevelt administration with Hitler's and Mussolini's regimes, they nevertheless identified in all three governments a seismic historical change from liberal to state capitalism, replete with a welfare state and government planning and direction of society. In 1944, Flynn prophesied that the policies of the New Deal would lead to ever increasing federal deficits. That in itself was not a problem as long as the populace could be kept content and state debts did not reach a critical mass. But willingly or unwillingly, Flynn argued, the New Deal had put itself in a position of needing a state of permanent crisis or, indeed, permanent war to justify its social interventions:

> It is born in crisis, lives on crises, and cannot survive the era of crisis. By the very law of its nature it must create for itself, if it is to continue, fresh crises from year to year. Mussolini came to power in the postwar crisis and became himself a crisis in Italian life. . . . Hitler's story is the same. And our future is all charted out upon the same turbulent road of permanent crisis.[1]

Flynn acknowledged explicitly that the United States would not necessarily, or even probably, go down the road of political repression, as Italy and Germany had. Instead, echoing the words of Gilbert H. Montague and Huey Long ten years earlier, he prophesied "a very genteel and dainty and pleasant form of fascism which cannot be called fascism at all because it will be so virtuous and polite."

*　　*　　*

THE PROBLEM WITH the New Deal–Fascism comparison of the 1930s (and all the America-as-Fascist constructs in post-Vietnam political rhetoric) has always been this concept of a "genteel" or "soft" American Fascism. A soft—that is, democratic—Fascism seems to be a contradiction in terms. But is it really? Didn't Tocqueville long ago warn against the leveling and conformist tendencies in American society? And aren't there entire passages in *Democracy in America* that read like precursors to Huxley's *Brave New World*, that classic of genteel totalitarianism?

That the comparison is made at all is surely due to the desire to explain a society so profoundly shaped by consensus. But the notion of "soft Fascism" does not in the end provide much illumination. A consideration of the question raised by Werner Sombart in 1906—"Why is there no socialism in the United States?"—may be of greater help in understanding what to the European mind sometimes appears as the enigma of American democracy. By the 1930s, commentators were asking the same question, this time with reference to socialism's archenemy: "Why is there no Fascism in the United States?" The answer in both cases was the same: neither socialism nor Fascism could take hold in the United States because Americans had no class consciousness. In Europe, class consciousness had been the driving force behind both movements. In the nineteenth century, socialism became the political creed of the working class; in the twentieth century, Fascism and National Socialism emerged as the rebellion of the middle class against socialism as well as capitalism. Their ingenious innovation was to declare themselves above and beyond class, a shift that explains their mass appeal and their ability to defame "old-style" socialism as serving the narrow interests of a single class.

As we have seen again and again, Fascism and National Socialism were "American" in their use of techniques of mass manipulation; we can now say that they were also American in their ideology of classlessness. The political, psychological, and charismatic leap needed to carry Fascism and National Socialism to power had been made in America under Andrew Jackson a century earlier, establishing classlessness as practically a civil religion. In their effort to create a classless folk-community, Fascism and National Socialism can be seen as attempts to modernize the Continent and raise it up to America's level. But influence flowed in the other direction as well. In its adoption of a social welfare system, the New Deal, it could be said, was carrying out a transformation that had taken effect in Europe, and first of all in Germany, fifty years previously. It is tempting to conjecture that a great swap occurred: While Fascist Europe took over the American creed of classlessness, New Deal America imported major elements of European economic and social order.

To extend this image, we might say that before the 1930s Europe and America were each in possession of only half of what was needed to create a modern mass society. Europe had its social welfare state yet remained mired in class struggle; America had its middle-class peace of mind but no system of social support. The crisis of the Depression made clear that neither ideology sufficed to hold society together. In Europe, the persistence of class struggle and class consciousness produced enormous social friction, while in the United States the absence of the lubricant of welfare-statism did much the same. But the imposition of Fascism in Europe was only achieved through violence, while the acceptance of state control in America was accomplished peacefully. This distinction may also be explained by the issue of class. To establish their version of a classless *Volksgemeinschaft* and *lo stato*, Fascism and National Socialism had to destroy the mighty infrastructure of class-consciousness: political parties, politicized unions, churches, and a widely ideologized sphere of culture and public opinion. The absence in America of both class-consciousness and its social, political, and cultural institutions made it relatively easy to persuade each individual in the mass of unorganized citizens that the actions of the state—represented by an authoritative you-and-me president—were undertaken for his or her personal benefit.

It was World War II that decided which system of statism would triumph in the global arena: the totalitarian welfare state along Fascist/National Socialist lines, or Roosevelt's liberal variant. As the outcome of the war demonstrated, Old Europe's bid to modernize via Fascism and National Socialism failed. The victor was America, but an America that achieved the stability that became its hallmark only by assimilating a major part of its defeated enemies' culture, much like the Alexandrian and Roman empires had in their time. The great postwar synthesis that created the trans-Atlantic "West," spanning the United States and Europe, would have been impossible without the cross-fertilization of the 1930s, which included, as Karl Mannheim gloomily predicted prior to the war, the ongoing influence of the totalitarian model:

> As soon as the Western states have taken up [the] funda-
> mental problem of universal security—the management
> of the trade cycle—they will gradually be forced to mani-
> pulate all social control, as the dictatorships have done
> from the start.... Competition with [the totalitarian]
> states compels the democracies to make use of some, at
> least, of their methods. [2]

It seems clear which of the two systems contributed more to the postwar West. Certainly at first glance, America seems to have exerted the dominant influence–especially in those countries that had gone through the "school" of Fascism/National Socialism. However, the fact that the American way of life was adopted in Germany and Italy more thoroughly and with less resistance than in, say, England and France, suggests that Fascism itself might have been a kind of preparatory training for this reeducation.

SINCE ITS DEFEAT in 1945 and subsequent departure from the center of the global stage, Europe has found itself in the comfortable situation of a prosperous rentier protected by its American guardian. The continent that had always been a military threat to the United States was transformed into an oasis of pacifism. On the other hand, America's own role changed profoundly as it assumed responsibility for the security of this European "Switzerland." In the words of Werner Sombart, the United States metamorphosed from *merchant* to *warrior*.

When Sombart used these terms during World War I to distinguish between mercantile England and bellicose Germany, the idea of the United States as a nation of warriors was close to inconceivable. Among the pillars of American national identity was the belief that the United States, in contrast to militaristic Europe, was a peacable republic of merchants, *pace* such figures as Teddy Roosevelt. This self-image was reversed with little fanfare during the forty years of the Cold War; official acknowledgment came only with the new doctrine of preventive war and its implementation in Iraq in 2003. That Germany—the militarist monster of the past, America' enemy in two World Wars, and since 1945, its most loyal ally—refused to participate in the invasion of Iraq made the exchange of roles powerfully clear. So did the American version of Sombart's merchant-warrior dichotomy, which held that America, acting self-confidently and aggressively, under the sign of *Mars*, had to distance itself and, if necessary, break with a "decadent" Europe that had fallen under the sway of hedonistic *Venus*.

Against the backdrop of such changed realities, Flynn's prognosis for the regime of his enemy Roosevelt sounds more apt today than when he originally made it in 1944, even though his reason—the cost of creating and maintaining the welfare state—is no longer a concern. "We must have enemies," he wrote in *As We Go Marching*, "They will become an economic necessity for us."

Notes

Introduction: On Comparisons

1. Sigfried Giedion, *Architectural Review*, September 1948, p. 126. There were, of course, isolated instances of self-criticism before then. Walter Gropius, for example, had already recognized, in his 1935 book *The New Architecture and the Bauhaus*, that the emphasis on rational functionality had led to one-sided formalism, although it was actually conceived merely as a "purifying agency," a means of freeing architecture from its stylistic excesses. See John Gloag, *Word Warfare* (London, 1939), p. 55.

2. See the anonymous commentary in the monthly journal edited by Bruno Zevi, *L'architettura*, June 1991, p. 504. Both Gavin Stamp in *Architectural Review*, November 9, 1991, p. 58, and the conference organizer Giorgio Ciucci in his book *Classicismo classicismi: Architettura Europa/America, 1920–1940* (Milan, 1995), p. 10, presume that the article was written by Zevi. In his book *Towards an Organic Architecture* (London, 1950), p. 49, Zevi described the neoclassicism of the 1930s as a symptom of "decadence" but blamed its rise as an architectural

style on the excessive formalism of modernism. In the wake of modernism's ossification, it is hardly surprising that representatives of so-called postmodern architecture have turned the accusation of totalitarianism around and directed it at modernism itself. Leon Krier, for example, writes, "Modernism has been the dominant style of totalitarian regimes left and right." See Krier's contribution to *New Classicism*, edited by A. Papadakis and H. Watson (New York, 1990), p. 6.

3. A number of recent works on the history of 1930s neoclassicism differentiate between political systems, national traditions, and individual architects. See Giorgio Ciucci, *Classicismo classicismi*; Ciucci, "Linguacci classicisti negli anni trenta in Europa e in America," in *L'estetica della politica: Europa e America negli anni trenta*, edited by Maurizio Vaudagna, Rome, 1989; Hartmut Frank, "Welche Sprache sprechen Steine?," *Faschistische Architekturen: Planen und Bauen in Europa, 1930–1945*, edited by Frank (Hamburg, 1985), pp. 7–21; and Franco Borsi, *The Monumental Era: European Architecture and Design, 1929–39* (New York, 1987).

4. Louis Craig et al., *The Federal Presence: Architecture, Politics, and Symbols in U.S. Government Building* (Cambridge, Mass., 1978), p. 331. See also Borsi, p. 196.

5. In the catalog to an exhibition celebrating the fiftieth anniversay of the Palais de Chaillot, Bertrand Lemoine writes that without its monumentalism, "the Exposition would neither have had the same presence nor have carried the same weight." The only building "able to stand up to the massiveness of the German and Soviet pavilions," the Palais was "neither a 'Nazi' nor a 'Mussolinian' monument; it conformed of course to an aesthetic of state representation, but with a modern, progressive ethic and the democratic and hedonistic values that go along with it. It must also be understood within the context of the global economic crisis that reinforced the role of the state as economic safe haven, provider of jobs in times of unemployment . . . [and] last resort of the destitute."

Lemoine goes on to contrast the "democratic" character of the Palais plaza with the Nazi parade grounds in Nuremberg: "No grand esplanade filled with the silence of immobilized crowds, the single voice amplified by loud speakers [but rather] a parvis open on two sides, a place of passage, of exchange, of pleasure: air and light, the hum of the city, the sight of the Seine, the Eiffel Tower and the Champs de Mars to be discovered as one stands at the parapet, leaning on one's elbows. This inspired space offers the public a belvedere, a theater from which to contemplate the landscape of Paris . . . a sight always the same, yet constantly renewed by the mood of the observer and the spectacle of the crowd." Bertrand Lemoine, "Le Palais de Chaillot," in *Paris 1937: Cinquantenaire de l'Exposition internationale des arts et des techniques dans la vie moderne* (Paris, 1987), pp. 98, 89.

The liberal British architecture critic John Gloag also noted the elements common to the aesthetic of state representation. Writing in 1939 about Albert Speer's new Imperial Chancellery, Gloag understood the building as a reaction to modernism, and described it in ways equally applicable to neoclassical buildings of the period in Paris, London, and Washington: "The wall is re-established as a barrier. It is no longer a skin, stretched lightly over steel bones: it has regained a medieval thickness of cuticle. The windows give the impression of being pierced in the wall, as though the building was first conceived as a strong box without apertures, and then, as an afterthought, or when it was safe to allow contact with the outer world, windows were traced, the thick stones cut through, the frames inserted." The effect of this architecture, Gloag adds, is an "empty calmness," which represents "something more than mere reaction from the modern movement, something more than a drawing-board itch to create a new 'style' gives these buildings power and strength and a touch of nobility. . . . They are a new order of architecture, a muscular order, expressing strength." From *Word Warfare*, pp. 40–41.

6. Cited in Robert C. Fried, *Planning the Eternal City* (New Haven, 1973), p. 32.

7. Cited in Timothy J. Colton, *Moscow: Governing the Socialist Metropolis* (Cambridge, Mass., 1995), p. 280.

8. Mussolini's most radical intervention in the cityscape of Rome was the Via del Impero, the boulevard between the Palazzo Venezia

(his residence) and the Colosseum, which was intended to symbolically connect the new regime with the Roman Empire.

9. John W. Reps, *Monumental Washington* (Princeton, 1967), p. 21.

10. Burnham's plan for Chicago, drawn up a few years after the one for Washington, has been compared to Albert Speer's vision of Germania. See Lars Olof Larsson, *Die Neugestaltung der Reichshauptstadt: Albert Speers Generalbebauungsplan für Berlin* (Stockholm, 1977), p. 116.

11. Reps, p. 194.

12. The two American studies on the topic are: Diane Ghirardo, *Building New Communities: New Deal America and Fascist Italy* (Princeton, 1989), and Leila Rupp, *Mobilizing Women for War: German and American Propaganda, 1939–45* (Princeton, 1978). Rupp obviously focuses on the period after the New Deal. In 1973, the German historian Heinrich August Winkler pointed out the need for "a comparative look at the period between the two world wars . . . which would shed light on the specific preconditions for the success of Fascist movements in Europe as well as the markedly different social and institutional frameworks that encouraged democratic solutions to problems in the Anglo-Saxon nations." See Winkler, *Die grosse Krise in Amerika* (Göttingen, 1973), p. 7. Winkler, however, did not himself pursue that line of research. Thirty years later, one of his students, Kiran Klaus Patel, published a dissertation comparing the Nazi Reichsarbeitsdienst with the American Civilian Conservation Corps. See Patel, *Soldaten der Arbeit* (Göttingen, 2003). There is also an unpublished master's thesis by Philipp Gassert comparing the job-creation programs in Germany and the United States. See Gassert, "Der New Deal in vergleichender Perspektive: Arbeitsbeschaffungsmassnahmen in den USA und im 3.Reich 1932–1935" (University of Heidelberg, 1990). Jürgen Kocka's pioneering work of comparative history, *Angestellte zwischen Faschismus und Demokratie: Zur politischen Sozialgeschichte der Angestellten USA 1890–1945 im internationalen Vergleich* (Göttingen, 1977), is less about the New Deal and Nazi governments than about class- and nation-specific social psychology. Italian scholars have taken

comparatively extensive interest in the connections between Fascism and the New Deal. Above all, Maurizio Vaudagna has made a name for himself in the field with numerous essays, his monograph *Corporativismo e New Deal* (Turin, 1981), and the compilation of essays *L'estetica della politica: Europa e America negli anni Trenta* (Rome, 1987), which he edited. Vaudagna's major articles include "Il corporativismo nel giudizio dei diplomatici americani a Roma, 1930–1935," *Studi storici*, vol. 3 (1975), pp. 764–96, and "New Deal e corporativismo nelle riviste politiche ed economiche italiane," in *Italia e America dalla Grande Guerra ad oggi*, edited by Giorgio Spini, Gian Giacomo Migone, and Massimo Teodori (Rome, 1976), pp. 110–40. Prior to Vaudagna, Franco Catalano wrote of the need for comparisons between Fascism and the New Deal in his article "New Deal e corporativismo fascista," *Il movimento di liberazione in Italia*, vol. 87 (1967). Catalano, however, never followed up with a comparison of his own.

13. John A. Garraty, "The New Deal, National Socialism, and the Great Depression," *American Historical Review*, vol. 78 (1973), pp. 907ff.

14. See Daniel Ritschel, "A Corporatist Economy in Britain? Capitalist Planning for Industrial Self-government in the 1930s," *English Historical Review* (1991), p. 47.

15. See B. Montagnon, A. Marquet, and M. Déat, *Néo-Socialisme?* (Paris, 1933). The neosocialists were excluded from the Socialist Party, but they continued to oppose Fascism until the end of the Third Republic. Under the Vichy regime, they then formed a Fascist party. Henri de Man's development in Belgium was similar, with the important difference being that far from representing a minority, he was the party leader. In his 1926 book *Au delà du marxisme*, de Man anticipated later criticisms of socialist parties as having exhausted their political strength. De Man was also among the first to call for socialism to reach out to the middle classes. See Zeev Sternhell, *Ni droite ni gauche: L'idéologie fasciste en France* (Paris, 1987), pp. 156ff.

16. See the section entitled "The Power of Symbols" in chapter 3, pp. 78–84.

17. Marcel Déat, "Socialisme et fascisme," *La grande revue* (August 1933), p. 191.

18. Murry, *Adelphi*, vol. 7, p. 329, and vol. 6, p. 245; see also Niebuhr, *Adelphi*, vol. 7, p. 199.

Chapter 1. Kinship?

1. The Fascist International of 1933–35 was an exclusively Italian project, an attempt by the first established Fascist power in Europe to secure its claim to historical importance and spiritual authority against National Socialism, whose rise had been greeted internationally with little understanding and even less enthusiasm. The driving force behind the project was the Fascist intelligentsia, with its Trotskyite leanings. Dismayed by the increasing bureaucratization of the Mussolini regime, Fascist intellectuals hoped that internationalism would provide the movement with new impulses and help realize their ideal of permanent revolution. Yet Michael Ledeen, a leading historian of the Fascist movement in Italy, calls the international conference, which was organized with great propagandistic fanfare in 1935 in a luxury hotel in Montreux, "a gigantic hoax." The delegates, he writes, were "a group of fascist, pseudo-fascist, and neo-fascist entrepreneurs, involved in the enterprise of soliciting funds from Rome for their own diversion and advancement." Ledeen, *Universal Fascism: The Theory and Practice of the Fascist International, 1928–1936* (New York, 1972), pp. 125–26.

2. The first three quotes are cited in Hans-Jürgen Schröder, *Deutschland und die Vereinigten Staaten, 1933–1939* (Wiesbaden, 1970), p. 93. The others are cited in Hans-Jürgen Schröder, "Das Dritte Reich und die USA," in *Die USA und Deutschland, 1918–1975,* edited by Manfred Knapp, Werner Link, Hans-Jürgen Schröder, and Klaus Schwabe (Munich, 1978), pp. 117–18; Harald Frisch, "Das deutsche Rooseveltbild (1933–1941)," Ph.D. diss., Free University of Berlin, 1967, p. 35; and Philipp Gassert, *Amerika im Dritten Reich* (Stuttgart, 1997), pp. 210–12.

3. Dodd cited in *Franklin D. Roosevelt and Foreign Affairs,* vol. 2

(Cambridge, Mass., 1969), p. 27. Wilson cited in *FDR and Foreign Affairs*, 2nd ser. (New York, 1995), vol. 9, pp. 21–22.

4. Cited in Frisch, p. 37, who also describes reports on America before 1936 as "a sphere free of manipulation" (p. 44). On the image of America in the German press during the first six months of National Socialism, see Kiran Patel, "Amerika als Argument: Die Wahrnehmung des New Deal am Anfang des 'Dritten Reiches,'" master's thesis, Humboldt University of Berlin; also in *Amerikastudien*, vol. 15, 2000. Backing the trend, writer Michael Freund, also the author of a biography of radical French syndicalist Georges Sorel, stressed the fundamental difference between the New Deal and National Socialism. At the same time as Europe's totalitarian nations were adopting an "American" optimism, Freund argued, the New Deal represented a trend in the United States toward pessimism: "A new future seemed to open up to the marching nations of Europe. The world seemed to grow wider, and they believed they were conquering uncharted territory like the 'pioneers.' The spirit of gigantic undertakings, which previously bore an American stamp, has seized nations like Italy and Russia. Meanwhile, the nation, which has just elected Roosevelt as its leader, is trying to get away from this Americanism." Freund, "Angelsächsische Revolution," *Deutsche Zeitschrift*, vol. 47 (1933–34), p. 252.

5. Bernard Fay, *Roosevelt and His America* (Boston, 1934), p. 310. One of the few foreign correspondents who saw the New Deal as having as much to do with National Socialism as with Fascism was the independent English socialist Fenner Brockway. Describing a visit to the United States in his book *Will Roosevelt Succeed?*, Brockway wrote that "the shouting, shrieking crowds, responding to the calls and antics of the cheerleaders, would fit exactly with the mass psychology of Fascist countries"; he added, "emotionally . . . America is nearer to Berlin and Moscow than to the deadly indifference of London." Calling the New Deal "a dictatorship by consent," he said that the cult of personality surrounding Roosevelt reminded him of German enthusiasm for Hitler. "Let me not be misunderstood," Brockway wrote. "I am not comparing the two men. I am comparing the similar methods adopted to arouse a similar psychology." The New Deal's propaganda methods,

he felt, went beyond even those applied in the Soviet Union: "Not even the propaganda of Moscow for the Five Years' Plan can be compared to this." And the labor camps of the Civilian Conservation Corps filled him with the same sense of foreboding as their equivalents in Germany: "One has the uneasy feeling that the American camps, no less than the German, would be transferred from civilian to military purposes immediately if war or a social uprising threatened." Cited from John Dizikes, *Britain, Roosevelt and the New Deal: British Opinion, 1932–1938* (New York, 1979), pp. 96, 166–67.

6. Hamilton Fish Armstrong, editor in chief of *Foreign Affairs* magazine, characterized National Socialism as "a twentieth-century revolution, as radical in its implications and potentialities as the Russian Revolution, but in the Prussian manner. . . . These young Nazis are proud to be ignorant. . . . Like young Soviet workers a few years ago in Russia, they are also proud to be free of the burdens of possessions. . . . Particles of the mass which is to rule the world, they are compelled forward by some cosmic urge." See Armstrong, "Hitler's Reich," *Foreign Affairs*, vol. 11 (June 1933), p. 595. On the divergent reception of Fascism and National Socialism, see Wolfgang Schieder, "Das italienische Experiment: Der Faschismus als Vorbild in der Krise der Weimarer Republik," *Historische Zeitschrift*, vol. 262 (1996), pp. 73–125. Schieder writes of a "philo-Fascist climate of opinion" (p. 84), which included even liberal German Jews such as Theodor Wolff and Emil Ludwig, both open admirers of Mussolini and committed opponents of Hitler. "In rejecting Hitler," Schieder writes, "one could express one's enthusiasm for Mussolini" and attempt to discredit National Socialism as "German pseudo-Fascism" (Schieder, p. 99).

7. Maurizio Vaudagna, "New Deal e corporativismo nelle riviste politiche ed economiche italiane," in *Italia e America dalla Grande Guerra a oggi*, edited by Giorgio Spini, Gian Giacomo Migone, and Massimo Teodori (Rome, 1976), p. 103.

8. The review appeared in *Popolo d'Italia* on July 7, 1933. Cited from Marco Sedda, "Il New Deal nella pubblicisticà politica italiana dal 1933 al 1938," *Il politico*, vol. 64 (1999), p. 250.

9. Maurizio Vaudagna, *Corporativismo e New Deal* (Turin, 1981), p. 201. Italy's ambassador in Washington, Augusto Rossi, reported back to Rome about the danger of "Italian self-celebration": "When our press rushed to portray Roosevelt as Mussolini's disciple . . . I had the feeling that insisting on this theme was not a good idea . . . it seemed to me that the word 'Fascism' would end up being used in party strife." See Vaudagna, "Mussolini and Roosevelt," in *Roosevelt and His Contemporaries*, edited by Cornelis A. van Minnen and John F. Sears (New York, 1992), p. 165.

10. Cited in Sedda, p. 263.

11. Ibid., p. 247.

12. Giovanni Selvi, "Fermentazione fascista nel mondo," *Gerarchia* (1935), pp. 576, 577.

13. See Sedda, pp. 251, 258, 265. An interesting corollary to the desire to link the New Deal with corporatism can be found in the Fascist attitudes toward the relationship between their own system and Soviet Communism. See Rosaria Quartararo, "Roma e Mosca: L'immagine dell'Urss nella stampa fascista, 1925–1935," *Storia contemporanea*, vol. 27 (1996), pp. 447–72. In contrast to National Socialism, which simply demonized Bolshevism, Italian Fascism between 1925 and 1935 made no secret of its interest in the Russian Communist experiment. Just as the New Deal was regarded as the first stage in America's adoption of a truly Fascist system, so, too, was Russian Bolshevism, in the words of the journal *Critica fascista*, seen as "the prelude to Fascism." Cited in Quartararo, p. 449. See also p. 452 for evidence that Italian Fascism's interest in Bolshevism began as early as 1922. Openness toward Bolshevism was motivated by foreign policy considerations. Until 1935, Mussolini pursued a successful strategy of trying to garner international weight as a mediator between East and West. The 1933 nonaggression pact between Rome and Moscow was part of this strategy, as was Italy's quick diplomatic recognition of the Soviet Union in the previous decade.

14. *Die deutsche Volkswirtschaft*, vol. 2 (1938), p. 75, and vol. 3 (1938), p. 100. German newspapers at the time were full of headlines such as "Roosevelt in a Corner," "Roosevelt's Dilemma," and "Roosevelt's

Worries." Prior to Roosevelt's 1937 foreign policy shift, the German media had tended to sympathize with Roosevelt as the victim of liberal constraints on his authority.

15. Hoover, *Addresses Upon the American Road* (New York, 1938), p. 160. "Too far" and "transplant" are cited in George Wolfskill and John A. Hudson, *All But the People: Franklin D. Roosevelt and His Critics, 1933–39* (London, 1969), p. 214.

16. Mauritz Hallgren: The first quotation is from the *Spectator* (August 18, 1933), p. 211. The second is cited in Arthur Ekirch, *Ideologies and Utopias: The Impact of the New Deal on American Thought* (Chicago, 1969), pp. 188–89.

17. Roger Shaw, "Fascism and the New Deal," *North American Review*, vol. 238 (1934), pp. 559, 562.

18. V. F. Calverton, "Will Fascism Come to America?," *Modern Monthly*, vol. 8 (1934), p. 472.

19. Ibid. p. 462. In *American Mercury*, George E. Sokolsky wrote, "Neither Mr. Roosevelt nor his Brain Trust has been guided by a full Fascist philosophy. They have no articulate philosophy. But their experiments are leading them into a Fascist position." Sokolsky, "America Drifts Toward Fascism," *American Mercury*, vol. 32 (1934), p. 259.

20. George Soule, *The Coming American Revolution* (New York, 1934), p. 294.

21. Oswald Garrison Villard, *Political Quarterly*, vol. 5 (1934), pp. 53–54.

22. J. B. Mathews and R. E. Shallcross, "Must America Go Fascist?," *Harper's Magazine*, vol. 169 (1934), p. 4.

23. Gilbert H. Montague, *Annals of the American Academy of Political and Social Sciences*, vol. 180 (1935), p. 159.

24. Norman Thomas, "Is the 'New Deal' Socialism? A Socialist Leader Answers," *New York Times*, June 18, 1933.

25. "Blood brothers": cited in Arthur M. Schlesinger, *The Politics of Upheaval*, vol. 3 of *The Age of Roosevelt* (Boston, 1960), p. 648. "These modern guilds": Franklin D. Roosevelt, *The Public Papers and Addresses*, vol. 2 (New York, 1938), p. 252.

26. See M. Vaudagna, "Mussolini and Roosevelt," in *Roosevelt and His Contemporaries*, p. 158.

27. Cited in John P. Diggins, *Mussolini and Fascism: The View from America* (Princeton, 1972), p. 279. On Long, see also Maurizio Vaudagna, "Il corporativismo nel giudizio dei diplomatici americani a Roma, 1930–1935," *Studi storici* (July–September 1975), pp. 772ff.

28. In her memoirs, Frances Perkins identifies the book as *The Corporate State* by Raffaelo Viglione, an assumption passed on by Arthur Schlesinger as fact in *The Coming of the New Deal* (vol. 2 of *The Age of Roosevelt* [Boston, 1959], p. 153). Since no book of this title exists, the volume in question is probably *The Italian Corporative State* by Fausto Pitigliani (London, 1933). Maurizio Vaudagna also cites an alleged letter to Johnson from Breckinridge Long, in which Long writes that the Italian corporations were organized "along the lines of the codes which you have been wrestling with" (Vaudagna, "Mussolini and Roosevelt," p. 164). There is no such letter in Johnson's estate, but Long did write a letter on the same date (May 16, 1934) to Rexford Tugwell, in which he said much the same thing: "Your mind runs along these lines [corporatism], and I think you might find some particular interest. . . . It may have some informative bearing on the Code work under N.R.A." (Long Papers, Box 111, Library of Congress, Manuscript Division).

29. *The Diary of Rexford G. Tugwell: The New Deal, 1932–1935*, edited by Michael Vincent Namorato (New York, 1992), pp. 138, 139. Tugwell's own account of a private discussion with America's ambassador to Germany, William Dodd, sheds light on Tugwell's political psychology. As Dodd expressed horror at Nazi barbarism, Tugwell understood the ambassador's point but considered it politically irrelevant: "I argued that when you unify a continent you automatically create internal political tensions which cause its government to concentrate on domestic matters and ignore foreign conquests" (p. 194). The technocrats who worked below the level of political decision making had no problem seeing the similarities between the NRA codes and Fascist corporatism. As one put it: "The Fascist Principles are very similar to those which we have been evolving here in America and so

are of particular interest at this time" (Janet C. Wright, "Capital and Labor Under Fascism," National Archives, Record Group 9, Records of the National Recovery Administration, Special Research and Planning Reports and Memoranda, 1933–35, Entry 31, Box 3).

30. *One Third of a Nation: Lorena Hickok Reports on the Great Depression*, edited by Richard Lowitt and Maurine Beasley (Urbana, 1981), p. 218.

31. Harold Ickes cited in Lewis S. Feuer, "American Travelers to the Soviet Union, 1917–32: The Formation of a Component of New Deal Ideology," *American Quarterly*, vol. 14 (1962). See also Kiran Klaus Patel, *Soldaten der Arbeit* (Göttingen, 2003), pp. 412–13, on Roosevelt's personal interest in the Nazi job creation ministry.

32. Peter Vogt, *Pragmatismus und Faschismus: Kreativität und Kontingenz in der Moderne* (Weilerswist, 2002). Vogt's use of the term "elective affinity" is somewhat bizarre since he actually argues that the two sides misunderstood each other. John P. Diggins, "Flirtation with Fascism: American Pragmatic Liberals and Mussolini's Italy," *American Historical Review*, vol. 71 (1966), p. 495.

33. "Conscious, intelligent" is from Diggins, p. 493. "Jefferson's fascism" is cited in Vogt, p. 56.

34. Cited in Diggins, p. 494.

35. With few exceptions, contemporary political and social scientists displayed little understanding of or sympathy for National Socialism. One writer who did understand was Californian political scientist William B. Munro, the author of a standard work on European systems of government and by no means a Nazi sympathizer. After a trip to Germany, Munro described Nazi anti-Semitism not as an irrational regression into medieval barbarism but as a reaction to the fact that "members of the Jewish race accumulated a good deal of economic power in pre-war Germany through their control of banking and credit as well as through the ownership of large industries, department stores, and newspapers." Munro, "Hitler and the New Deal in Germany," *Proceedings of the Institute of World Affairs* (Los Angeles, 1934); reprinted in *The Governments of Europe* (New York, 1938), p. 634.

36. The authorship of this quote is unclear. Arthur Schlesinger attributes it to 1930s journalist Lawrence Dennis, who was often, mistakenly, accused of being a Fascist himself. Schlesinger quotes Dennis: "Nothing could be more logical or in the best political tradition than for a type of fascism to be ushered into this country by leaders who are now vigorously denouncing fascism." Schlesinger, see note 25, above, p. 665. In 1936 the *Journal of Social Psychology* took a poll aimed at establishing the latent Fascist tendencies of the American populace. While the vast majority of respondents described themselves as anti-Fascist, they also expressed support for Fascist views so long as these were not explicitly identified as such. *Journal of Social Psychology*, vol. 7 (1936), pp. 309–19, 438–54.

Among the most well known of the movements that did exist was the "Silver Shirts," a Protestant militia formed in 1933 by journalist William Dudley Pelley to fight Communism. But it was never more than a tiny fringe group. If we follow the logic of sociologist Werner Sombart, the reason for its failure was evident: collective movements had little chance in a nation that considered itself the founder of individualism. There was another category of spontaneous, catchall movements that formed around radical public figures, which many commentators at the time considered latently, if not explicitly, Fascist; in the mid-1930s, these movement represented a serious challenge to the New Deal. The populist demagoguery of "radio priest" Charles E. "Father" Coughlin and Louisiana governor and senator Huey Long— both early supporters and later vehement detractors of FDR—is today considered to be the true American equivalent of European Fascism and National Socialism.

37. Leon Samson, "Is Fascism Possible in America?," *Common Sense* (August 1934), p. 17. One of Samson's examples is the institution of the presidency: "The President here is the tribune of the people. As such he embodies, at one and the same time, the form of democracy and the substance of Caesarism. . . . It is precisely in his role as spokesman of the mass against the class that the American President performs the function of fascism without assuming any of its forms."

Another differentiating element is the pace of American life: "American tempo acts in a truly fascist manner to override everything historically ordered and real, opening the door to a dilletantism (*sic!*) of power—that chief spiritual component of the fascist style of life" (p. 18). Analysis of social conformism within the American ideology of individualism has a long tradition among European observers, from Tocqueville to what one Italian historian has recently called "the paradox of conformist democracy." See Daria Frezza, *Il leader, la folla, la democrazia nel discorso pubblico americano, 1880–1941* (Rome, 2001). John Maynard Keynes formulated this idea in the 1930s, opining, "Americans are apt to be unduly interested in discovering what average opinion believes average opinion to be." *The General Theory* (New York, 1936), p. 159. As the more recent idea of political correctness makes evident, this sort of conformity is the result of an ostensibly voluntary process, whereby political insight leads everyone to hold the same opinion. The tendency in English to speak of ideas being "bought" and "sold" helps us better understand the psychology of this relationship, which only works because both sides are dependent on each other. European observers have identified a similar psychology at work in American behavior in street traffic: "The result is a sense of security on the roads we can only dream of." Hyacinthe Dubreuil, *Les codes Roosevelt: Les perspectives de la vie sociale* (Paris, 1934), p. 135.

38. Waldo Frank, "Will Fascism Come to America?," *Modern Monthly*, vol. 8 (1934), pp. 465–66.

39. E. Francis Brown, "The American Road to Fascism," *Current History* (July 1933), p. 397.

40. W. P. Montague, "Democracy at the Crossroads," in Actes du huitième congrès international de philosophie à Prague, 2-7 *septembre 1934* (Prague 1936), p. 481.

41. Cited from William E. Leuchtenburg, "The New Deal and the Analogue of War," in *The FDR Years: On Roosevelt and His Legacy* (New York, 1995), pp. 35–75.

42. On Swope's plan and the NRA, see Kim McQuaid, *A Response to Industrialism: Liberal Businessmen and the Evolving Spectrum of Capitalist*

Reform, 1880–1960 (New York, 1986). See also McQuaid and Edward Berkowitz, *Creating the Welfare State* (New York, 1980), and David Loth, *Swope of G.E.* (New York, 1958).

43. Richard T. Ely, *Hard Times: The Way in and the Way Out* (New York, 1931), p. 103.

44. Vaudagna, *L'estetica*, p. 97 (see Introduction, n. 3).

45. Cited in Daniel R. Fusfeld, *The Economic Thought of FDR and the Origins of the New Deal* (New York, 1956), p. 50.

46. See Richard Hofstadter, *The Age of Reform* (New York, 1955); Arthur A. Ekirch, *Progressivism in America* (New York, 1974), and Robert Miewald, "The Origins of Wilson's Thought: The German Tradition and the Organic State," in *Politics and Administration*, edited by J. Rabin and J. Bowman (New York, 1984).

47. Insofar as they were not subject to censorship, critics at the time also expressed fears that the United States was headed down a path of Prussian autocracy in its struggle against Prussian militarism. William Dodd, America's future ambassador to Germany, warned that Wilson "would be compelled to adopt the very programme which Bismarck had employed in the building of imperialist Germany." In an article entitled "Are We in Danger of Becoming Prussianized?," economist Thomas N. Carver wrote, "Already, in our war, along with the increased use of governmental authority has come a corresponding centralization of power. Centralization, carried to its logical and efficient extreme, results in Caesarism, Bonapartism, bureaucracy, Prussianism. However democratic the authoritarian may think that he is, or pretend to be, the very nature of his programme carries him logically and unavoidably toward that centralization of power which the world now calls Prussianism." Cited in Arthur A. Ekirch, *Progressivism in America* (New York, 1974), pp. 271, 273. Robert Nisbeth called two of Wilson's "enabling acts" (the Espionage Act and the Sedition Act) "the West's first real experience with totalitarianism—political absolutism extended into every possible area of culture and society, education, religion, industry, the arts, local community and family included, with a kind of terror always waiting in the wings—[this] came with the American war state under Woodrow Wilson." Nisbeth, *Twilight of*

Authority (New York, 1975), p. 183. On another occasion Nisbeth said, "Though we are loath to admit it, the first twentieth-century preview of the totalitarian state was provided by the United States in 1917–18. . . . Not even the Kaiser's military-political order, much less that of either England and France, reached the totality of the war-state that America did." Nisbeth, *The Making of Modern Society* (Brighton, Eng., 1986), p. 192.

48. Cited in Allen F. Davis, "Welfare, Reform and World War I," *American Quarterly*, vol. 19 (1967), pp. 519, 520, 521.

Chapter 2. Leadership

1. Marquis de La Londe, "L'expérience américaine: La popularité du Président Roosevelt," *La revue mondiale* (September 1–15, 1935), p. 4.

2. Cited from the German edition: Hendrik de Man, *Massen und Führer* (Potsdam, 1932), pp. 43, 44.

3. Alexandre Dorna, *Le leader charismatique* (Paris, 1998), pp. 26–27.

4. Erich Becker, *Diktatur und Führung* (Tübingen, 1935), p. 35.

5. Roger Bonnard, *Le droit et l'État dans la doctrine nationale-socialiste* (Paris, 1936), pp. 92, 94.

6. Hadley Cantril and Gordon W. Allport, *The Psychology of the Radio* (New York, 1935; repr., New York, 1971), p. 109.

7. Betty H. Winfield, *FDR and the News Media* (Urbana, 1990), p. 105. On FDR's radio addresses in particular, see Robert S. Fine, "Roosevelt's Radio Chatting: Its Development and Impact During the Great Depression," Ph.D. diss., New York University, 1977. Fine (p. 127) cites a 1937 analysis by the *New York Times* of FDR's vocabulary, which concluded that 70 percent of the time FDR used only the five hundred most common words in the English language.

8. Cited in Orrin Dunlap, "When Roosevelt Gets on the Air," *New York Times* (June 18, 1933).

9. Winfield, p. 105.

10. John Dos Passos, *Common Sense* (February 1934), p. 17.

11. Dunlap, ibid. Bernard Fay, "La campagne électorale aux États-Unis," *Revue des deux mondes* (December 1, 1936), p. 614.

12. See Fay, ibid.: "Never a great orator, one of those men whom contact with the crowd lifts above themselves, he lost nothing for being on the radio; on the contrary, because his great art was that of witty conversation—informal, subtle, and intimate—he seems to have been born for the radio."

13. Warren Susman, *Culture as History* (New York, 1984), p. 160.

14. Cited in Arthur M. Schlesinger Jr., *The Coming of the New Deal*, vol. 2 of *The Age of Roosevelt* (Boston, 1959), p. 572.

15. Ernst Hanfstaengl, *Zwischen Weissem und Braunem Haus: Memoiren eines politischen Aussenseiters* (Munich, 1970), pp. 36–39. Today's analysts agree. "When speaking calmly, his deep baritone voice could reach the high tenor register without becoming falsetto. It remained a chest voice. Hitler did not just vary his volume, a key technique in effective rhetorical oratory. He also exploited the seductive, melodic quality of his voice in its deeper, warmer registers. All in all, the impression is one of total expressiveness without monotony, a perfect mixture for suggestively influencing his audience." Karl-Heinz Göttert, *Geschichte der Stimme* (Munich, 1998), p. 439.

16. Ulrich Ulonska, *Suggestion der Glaubwürdigkeit: Untersuchungen zu Hitlers rhetorischer Selbstdarstellung zwischen 1920 und 1933* (Hamburg, 1990), p. 286.

17. Ibid., pp. 97, 103. Ironically, Hitler's oratorical style was also likely influenced by that of leading socialist politicians in Munich during the ill-fated Bavarian revolution in the winter of 1918–19. Otto Zarek, a witness to that event, later drew a comparison between the rhetoric of Hitler and of socialist leader and playwright Ernst Toller: "It was not Toller's matter but his manner that finally won his hearers. People couldn't make up their minds whether he was right or not, but they had no doubt that he was sincere. . . . He carried the people by the force of his own convictions. . . . When he went on to explain that their case was the case of mankind . . . the little man from the suburbs felt flattered and applauded loudly. . . . They wanted a mission in life;

Toller supplied them with one." Cited in Sterling Fishman, "The Rise of Hitler as Beerhall Orator," *Review of Politics*, vol. 26 (1964), p. 249.

18. Joachim Fest, *Hitler* (Berlin, 1995), p. 217.

19. Detlef Grieswelle, *Propaganda der Friedlosigkeit: Eine Studie zu Hitlers Rhetorik 1920–1933* (Stuttgart, 1972), p. 43.

20. A French eyewitness to one of Hitler's appearances described the crowd as "by dint of waiting . . . already drunk on itself." Pierre Frédérix, "Hitler, manieur de foule," *Revue des deux mondes* (March 1, 1934), p. 65. On the psychology of waiting, see French sociologist Marcel Mauss: "Waiting is one of those events in which emotion, perception, and, to be more exact, the motion and state of the body directly condition the social state and are themselves conditioned by it. . . . Waiting brings about a thrilling fusion of the leader and his supporters: they identify charismatically with him while he realizes himself narcissistically through them. When they believe they perceive in him their much awaited hopes, it is then that an internal, one might even say a 'psycho-physiological,' change takes place." Cited in Dorna, p. 29. Roosevelt's fireside chats also built up listeners' expectations, albeit in different form, insofar as hourly promotional announcements were broadcast throughout the days in question. See John A. Sharon, "The Psychology of the Fireside-Chat," Ph.D. diss., Princeton University, 1949, p. 95.

21. Cited in Claudia Schmölders, *Hitlers Gesicht* (Munich, 2000), p. 54.

22. Fest, p. 448.

23. Eitel W. Dobert, cited in F. W. Lambertson, "Hitler, the Orator: A Study in Mob Psychology," *Quarterly Journal of Speech*, vol. 28 (1942), p. 124.

24. Otto Strasser, cited in Lambertson, p. 127.

25. James G. MacDonald, chairman of the Foreign Policy Association, in a speech in New York on May 4, 1933. Summarized by German ambassador Hans Luther (Polit. Arch. AA, R 80307, Blatt K 269124).

26. Cited in Grieswelle, p. 39.

27. Konrad Heiden, *Hitler* (New York, 1936), p. 304.

28. Theodor Adorno, "Freudian Theory and the Pattern of Fascist Propaganda," in *The Culture Industry: Selected Essays on Mass Culture* (London, 1991). Adorno applied these ideas not just to Hitler but also to figures like Huey Long and Father Coughlin, whose movements he characterized as the American equivalents of European Fascism. Harold Lasswell, the leading American social psychologist and propaganda expert of the 1920s and '30s, offered a related, if more down-to-earth explanation for the führer's popularity in his 1933 essay "The Psychology of Hitlerism": "Hitler's role resembles that of the nurse who tells her crying charge that the neighbor boy was very naughty to hit him." *Political Quarterly*, vol. 4, p. 380. In an often-quoted remark, Hitler himself described the masses as a "woman," which fit well with his own self-conception as leader. Yet as we have seen, the "masculine," aggressive part of his speeches proceeded only after a harmonious, "feminine" introduction. Joachim Fest (p. 186) writes of Hitler's "unusual, feminine-seeming sensitivity" for the moods and desires of the masses.

29. Particularly worth mentioning in this context are the illustrated books by Hitler's favorite photographer, Heinrich Hoffmann. These works, with titles such as *The Unknown Hitler* (1932) and *Hitler in His Mountains* (1935), were published after the führer had achieved mass popularity and aimed to give readers the impression of knowing the "private Hitler." See *Hoffmann & Hitler: Photographie als Medium des Führermythos*, edited by Rudolf Herz (Munich, 1994).

30. Hadley Cantril and Gordon W. Allport, *The Psychology of the Radio* (New York, 1935; repr., New York, 1971), p. 13.

31. Cited in Eugene E. Leach, "Mastering the Crowd: Collective Behaviour and Mass Society in American Social Thought, 1917–1939," *American Studies* (1986), p. 109.

32. Susman, p. 165.

33. Franco Minganti, *Modulazioni de frequenza: L'immaginario radiofonico tra letteratura e frequenza* (Pasian di Prato, 1997), p. 35.

34. Eckhard Breitinger, *Rundfunk und Hörspiel in den USA, 1930–1950* (Trier, 1992), pp. 79, 78, 86.

35. Cited in James Thurber's essay "Soapland," in Thurber, *The Beast in Me and Other Animals* (New York, 1968), p. 254.

36. David Welch, *The Third Reich: Politics and Propaganda* (London, 1993), p. 34.

37. Ibid., p. 33.

Chapter 3. Propaganda

1. Max Lerner, "The Pattern of Fascism," *Yale Review*, vol. 24 (1934), p. 310.

2. Harold D. Lasswell, "The Person: Subject and Object of Propaganda," *Annals of the American Academy of Political and Social Science*, vol. 179 (1935), p. 189.

3. Cited in Fritz Morstein Marx, "Propaganda and Dictatorship," *Annals of the American Academy of Political Science* (May 1935), p. 212. There is some uncertainty about whether the quote is genuine, but Ernest K. Bramsted also quotes a similar statement by Goebbels: "It was imperative to keep a finger on the fluctuating pulse of the masses if propaganda was not to be carried out in a void . . . to be close to the changing moods of the people to understand them in order to be able to persuade and indoctrinate them." *Goebbels and National Socialist Propaganda, 1925–1945* (Michigan, 1965), pp. 53–54.

4. Richard W. Steele, "The Pulse of the People: Franklin D. Roosevelt and the Gauging of American Public Opinion," *Journal of Contemporary History*, vol. 9 (1974), p. 203. See also Steele, "Preparing the Public for War: Efforts to Establish a National Propaganda Agency," *American Historical Review*, vol. 75 (Oct. 1970).

5. On the plebiscitary element within the fireside chats, see Thomas Vernor Smith, "The New Deal as Cultural Phenomenon," in *Ideological Differences and World Order*, edited by F. S. C. Northrop (New Haven, 1949), p. 225.

6. Garraty, pp. 932, 925 (see Introduction, n. 13).

7. Elisha Hanson, "Official Propaganda and the New Deal," *Annals of the American Academy of Political and Social Science*, vol. 179 (1935), p. 178.

8. Daria Frezza, "Democrazia e mass media: Il New Deal e l'opinione pubblica," in *Ripensare Roosevelt*, edited by Tiziano Bonazzi and Maurizio Vaudagna (Milan, 1986), p. 226.

9. William E. Berchtold, "Press Agents of the New Deal," *New Outlook* (July 1934), p. 24.

10. Kiran Klaus Patel, "Die Edition der 'NS-Presseanweisungen' im Kontext von Quellensammlungen zum 'Dritten Reich,'" *Archiv für Sozialgeschichte*, vol. 42 (2002), p. 369. As is typical of dictatorial systems, the official Nazi press, confident of its position, often took greater liberties than the nominally independent media. Patel adds that "the Nazi press more often deviated from party rules on acceptable speech" and "that the formerly anti-Nazi media stuck closer to guidelines than many regime-friendly publications."

11. See Culbert's essay in *Führerbilder: Hitler, Mussolini, Roosevelt, Stalin in Fotografie und Film*, edited by Martin Loiperdinger, Rudolf Herz, and Ulrich Pohlmann (Munich, 1995), pp. 168, 171–72.

12. See Richard W. Steele, *Propaganda in an Open Society: The Roosevelt Administration and the Media, 1933–1940* (Westport, Conn., 1985), pp. 18–20.

13. Franz Springer, "Die politischen Prinzipien des Rundfunkrechts in den Vereinigten Staaten von Amerika, Italien, England und Sowjetrussland," Ph.D. diss., Erlangen, 1935).

14. See Steele, *Propaganda*, pp. 128ff., 18–24. He concludes, "Broadcasters sought safety from potentially harmful intervention by proving their value to those in power. . . . Everything the Administration had to say went over the airwaves without the intercession of reporters, editors, or publishers" (p. 20).

15. Cited in Fest, pp. 187–88 (see chap. 2, n. 18). See also a similar passage in Adolf Hitler, *Mein Kampf* (Munich, 1943), p. 193: "I saw [in propaganda] an instrument that the Socialist-Marxist parties themselves had used with masterful skill."

16. Hitler, ibid., p. 552.

17. Edward L. Bernays, "Molding Public Opinion," *Annals of the American Academy of Political Science*, p. 84; Lasswell, p. 189.

18. See Richard Albrecht, "Symbolkampf in Deutschland 1932: Sergej Tschachotin und der 'Symbolkrieg' der drei Pfeile gegen den Nationalsozialismus als Episode im Abwehrkampf der Arbeiterbewegung gegen den Faschismus in Deutschland," *Internationale Wissenschaftliche Korrespondenz zur Geschichte der deutschen Arbeiterbewegung,* vol. 22 (1966), pp. 498–535, and Karl Rohe, *Das Reichsbanner Schwarz Rot Gold: Ein Beitrag zur Geschichte und Struktur der politischen Kampfverbände zur Zeit der Weimarer Republik* (Düsseldorf, 1966).

19. See Albrecht, p. 506. Marxist philosopher Ernst Bloch leveled a similar criticism at his peers' response to National Socialism in 1937: "I have nothing against the material *logos* or the dialectic of materialism, but human beings aren't made of stone. The revolution does not just take hold of man's reason, but also of his imagination, which socialists have long under-fed. . . . The Nazis have lied, but they lied to people, while socialists have told the truth but only about abstract things. It's time to tell the people the truth about things that matter to them." "Kritik der Propaganda," *Neue Weltbühne* (May 25, 1937), p. 553.

20. Fireside chat on July 24, 1933.

21. Cited in Schlesinger, *The Coming of the New Deal*, p. 114 (see chap. 2, n. 14).

22. Cited in Andrew Davis Wolvin, "The 1933 Blue Eagle Campaign: A Study in Persuasion and Coercion," Ph.D. diss., Purdue University, 1968, p. 51.

23. Estimates of the numbers of volunteers involved in the Blue Eagle campaign range as high as 1.5 million. See Ernst Basch, *Das Wiederaufbauwerk Roosevelts* (Zurich, 1935), p. 110.

24. John Kennedy Ohl, *Hugh S. Johnson and the New Deal* (Dekalb, Ill., 1985), pp. 140, 106, 102.

25. Cited in Hugh S. Johnson, *The Blue Eagle from Egg to Earth* (New York, 1935), pp. 154–55.

26. Cited in Garraty, p. 930 (see Introduction, n. 13).

27. Cited in Wolvin, pp. 194–95.

28. Ibid., p. 197.

29. Anne O'Hare McCormick, a Roosevelt supporter, described

the Blue Eagle campaign as "an educational agency, forcing those within and without the codes to do some hard thinking on the central problems of modern life." *New York Times Magazine* (July 8, 1934).

30. Wolvin, p. 221.

31. William E. Berchtold, "The World Propaganda War," *North American Review*, vol. 238 (1934), p. 429. With reference to Joseph Goebbels, Berchtold adds, "Many a minister of propaganda could afford to take a few pages out of the Roosevelt notebook" (p. 428).

32. Ethan Colton, *Four Patterns of Revolution: Communist USSR, Fascist Italy, Nazi Germany, New Deal America* (New York, 1935), p. 270. Yet Colton qualifies that judgment, writing, "But [the New Deal] lacked their fighting spirit. Comparatively, the response was feeble. The effort to create a crusading mentality failed. The dollar and cents objectives called forth neither sacrifice nor heroism."

33. *Economist*, September 9, 1933; *Spectator*, September 22, 1933.

34. Cited in John Dizikes, *Britain, Roosevelt and the New Deal: British Opinion, 1932–1938* (New York, 1979), p. 163.

35. Robert de Saint-Jean, *La vraie révolution de Roosevelt* (Paris, 1934), p. 51. Marquis de La Londe was so impressed by the theatrical image for the campaign that he quoted this passage word for word, but without attribution, in an article for *La revue mondiale* (September 1–15, 1935), p. 4.

36. Simone-Maxe Benoit, *Revue politique et littéraire*, vol. 164 (July 1935), p. 59.

37. de La Londe, p. 3.

38. Louis Rosenstock-Franck, *L'Expérience Roosevelt et le milieu social américain* (Paris, 1937), p. 115.

39. Bernard Fay, "Deux ans d'expérience Roosevelt," *Revue des deux mondes* (March 1, 1935), pp. 37–38. An earlier article in the Swiss daily *Neue Zürcher Zeitung* (September 3, 1933) made the same point: "It has already proved necessary to appeal not just to feelings of national enthusiasm but also to feelings of fear."

40. Fritz Morstein Marx, *Government in the Third Reich* (London, 1937), p. 96.

41. Lasswell, p. 360.

42. Cited in "Opferritual und Volksgemeinschaft am Beispiel des Winterhilfswerks," in *Faschismus und Ideologie, 2.Sonderband "Das Argument"* (Berlin, 1980); Herwart Vorländer, "NS-Volkswohlfahrt und Winterhilfswerk des deutschen Volkes," *Vierteljahresschrift für Zeitgeschichte*, vol. 34 (1986), pp. 365ff.; Florian Tennstedt, "Wohltat und Interesse: Das Winterhilfswerk des deutschen Volkes—die Weimarer Vorgeschichte und ihre Instrumentalisierung durch das NS-Regime," *Geschichte und Gesellschaft*, vol. 13 (1987), p. 174ff.

43. Aryeh Unger, "Propaganda and Welfare in Nazi Germany," *Journal of Social History*, vol. 4 (1970–71), p. 136. At the same time, the men behind the Blue Eagle campaign and the Winter Relief Organization also explicitly discouraged the rank and file from undertaking vigilante reprisals against nonparticipants. See Unger, p. 138.

44. The phrase occurs in a letter from Keynes to Roosevelt. See Richard Adelstein, "The Nation as an Economic Unit: Keynes, Roosevelt and the Managerial Ideal," *Journal of American History*, vol. 78 (1991), p. 177.

45. Pierre Frédérix, "Hitler, manieur des foules," *Revue des deux mondes* (March 1, 1934), p. 63.

46. The term "regime" is used here in historian Peter Temin's sense: "The regime is an abstraction from any single decision; it represents the systematic and predictable part of all decisions. It is the thread that runs through the individual choices that governments and central banks have to make." *Lessons from the Great Depression* (Cambridge, Mass., 1989), p. 91.

47. According to Temin, society could be mobilized to fight the economic crisis only through "dramatic and highly visible... symbols of the change that could be widely understood." Ibid., p. 92. On Roosevelt's "tendency to substitute fighting words and symbolic deeds for more substantive action," see Paul Conkin, *FDR and the Origins of the Welfare State* (New York, 1976); and Conkin and David Burner, *A History of Recent America* (New York, 1974), pp. 236–37, 243, 248. On the preponderance of symbol over substance in Roosevelt's tax reforms, see Mark H. Leff, *The Limits of Symbolic Reform: The New Deal and Taxation, 1933–1939* (New York, 1984).

48. Hartmut Berghoff, "Enticement and Deprivation: The Regulation of Consumption in Pre-War Nazi Germany," in *Material Culture and Citizenship in Europe and America*, edited by Martin Daunton and Matthew Hilton (Oxford, 2000), p. 167.

49. See Thomas Vernor Smith, "The New Deal as a Cultural Phenomenon," in *Ideological Differences and World Order: Studies in the Philosophy and Science of the World Cultures*, edited by F. S. C. Northrop (New Haven, 1949), p. 208ff. Warren Susman traces the emphasis on games back to the novel, technological quality of the culture industry, in particular to cinema, radio, and sports, and to the increasing popularity of gambling. These developments not only reflected the Depression-era need for escapism but also represented opportunities "to maintain and reinforce essential values, to keep alive a sense of hope. . . . The increase in the particular kind of games that did dominate . . . life in the '30s tended to provide significant social reinforcement. Even the dances marked a return to an almost folk-style pattern of large-scale participation and close cooperation." *Culture as History*, p. 162 (see chap. 2, n. 13).

50. Perkins cited in Smith, p. 227. Chase, *A New Deal* (New York, 1932), p. 252.

51. Roger Caillois, *Man, Play and Games* (Urbana and Chicago, 2001), p. 55.

Chapter 4. Back to the Land

1. See Alexius Boér Jr., "Die internationalen Goldbewegungen," *Weltwirtschaftliches Archiv*, vol. 31 (1930), p. 462. The psychological dependence on gold was most persistent in France, with its strong culture of private investment; people believed that any deviation from the gold standard would plunge the system into immediate ruin. Even as late as 1969 Charles de Gaulle would proclaim that gold reserves were necessary to ensure the "stability, impartiality and universal validity" of the franc. Yet as Keynes was the first to realize, a change in psychology was needed before capital could be freed from the restrictions

placed on aggressive financial and investment policies by the gold standard. Only after this had been achieved could those new relations arise between the state, the economy, and consumer society that have determined the economy and culture of the West since 1945. In our eyes today, gross domestic product, coupled with a nation's capacity for consumption, is what guarantees the stability and security of its currency. The psychology of economic self-sufficiency and the soil in the 1930s is an often forgotten transitional phase between the gold and the consumer ages. This was true even for the United States, which had the world's largest stocks of gold. Indeed, the transfer of America's gold reserves in 1936 from New York City to Fort Knox can be seen as a symbolic act, in which the wealth of the people was taken out of the hands of previously all-powerful urban plutocrats and restored to the bosom of the nation.

2. Ferdinand Fried, *Wende der Weltwirtschaft* (Leipzig, 1939), p. 387.

3. Ferdinand Fried, *Autarkie* (Jena, 1932), p. 42. Fried's colleague Bernhard Laum also criticized the destruction of the "organic" unity of the preliberal economy and the creation of harmful "extremes" by global commerce and the global-economic division of labor. "Death lies at the extremes," Laum wrote. "Preservation of life lies only in the middle"—i.e., in an "organic" system of national autarky. *Die geschlossene Wirtschaft: Soziologische Grundlegung des Autarkieproblems* (Tübingen, 1933), p. 466.

4. See Susman, pp. 211–12 (see chap. 2, n. 13).

5. This side of Marx has been developed in recent years by ecological Marxism. In this interpretation, Marx saw the capitalist exploitation of nature as parallel to the capitalist exploitation of the proletariat. Ecological Marxists stress passages in the late writings that express a preference for small private farmers, who were tied to their land through bonds of "natural" empathy, over "insensitive" large industrial-style agriculture. See John Bellamy Foster, *Marx's Ecology: Materialism and Nature* (New York, 2000), p. 165. See also Paul Burkett, *Marx and Nature: A Red and Green Perspective* (New York, 1999).

6. Le Corbusier cited in Mary McLeod, "Urbanism and Utopia: Le Corbusier from Regional Syndicalism to Vichy," Ph.D. diss., Princeton University, 1988, pp. 299, 312.

7. Ford cited in Reynold M. Wik, *Henry Ford and Grass-Roots America* (Ann Arbor, 1972), p. 192. "Cars sprouting": Helmut Magers, *Roosevelt: Ein Revolutionär aus common sense* (Leipzig, 1934), p. 112.

8. Egon Bandmann in *Deutsche Zukunft* (December 23, 1934), p. 13; Stuart Chase cited in Arthur M. Schlesinger Jr., *The Crisis of the Old Order, 1919–1933*, vol. 1 of *The Age of Roosevelt* (Boston, 1957), p. 201.

9. Stuart Chase, *Mexico: A Study of Two Americas* (1931; repr., New York, 1946), pp. 310–11.

10. Ibid., pp. 323–24.

11. Cited by Jean-Louis Cohen, in *Faschistische Architekturen*, edited by Hartmut Frank (Hamburg, 1985), p. 205.

12. Historian Mechtild Rössler writes, "Self-management and independent responsibility in joint projects between universities were basic components of this new idea of academic research. There was no direct pressure from National Socialist political offices or the party. No demands were made from the 'outside.'" Rössler, "Die Institution-alisierung einer neuen 'Wissenschaft' im Nationalsozialismus: Raum-forschung und Raumordnung 1935–1945," *Geographische Zeitschrift*, vol. 75 (1987), p. 181. In the United States, "regional planning" was already an academic discipline, but it first became part of government policy as part of the New Deal.

13. Ibid., pp. 186, 182; emphasis in original.

14. Cited in David R. Conrad, *Education for Transformation: Implications in Lewis Mumford's Ecohumanism* (Palm Springs, 1976), p. 110.

15. *American Regionalism*, edited by Howard W. Odum with Harry Estill Moore (New York, 1938), p. 12 (Lewis), p. 28 (Mumford), pp. 3, 639–40 (Odum).

16. Odum: ibid., p. 637. Elliott: William Yandell Elliott, *The Need for Constitutional Reform* (New York, 1935), pp. 191–93.

17. "Garden-city socialism" was in part inspired by utopian novels

that appeared in the 1890s: Edward Bellamy's *Looking Backward*, William Morris's *News from Nowhere*, and Peter Kropotkin's *Fields, Factories and Workshops; or, Industry Combined with Agriculture and Brain Work with Manual Work*. They depicted postcapitalistic worlds in which divisions between town and country were reconciled by dissolving urban-industrial society into rural-industrial idylls.

18. In Germany many of the architects associated with this development (including modernist icon Bruno Taut) were the same men who had wanted to replace the city with the garden city immediately after World War I—and who then, in the mid-1920s, converted to the cult of the city that was a central part of the New Objectivity. See Tilman Harlander, *Zwischen Heimstätte und Wohnmaschine* (Basel and Boston, 1995), p. 33.

19. Paul Conkin, *Tomorrow a New World: The New Deal Community Program* (Ithaca, 1959), pp. 239–40.

20. Ibid., p. 246ff.

21. Ibid., p. 118.

22. Diane Ghirardo, *Building New Communities: New Deal America and Fascist Italy* (Princeton, 1989), p. 181. Ghirardo, one of the few scholars to compare this segment of American and European history, also writes, "In the kind of control exerted by the government, American cooperatives differed dramatically from state-initiated cooperatives in Germany and Italy, where, once having completed the buildings, the government stepped out of the picture except when called in to arbitrate disputes. In their day-to-day operation American cooperatives revealed a pronounced drive to implement drastic social changes through the cooperatives by means of paternalistic and ultimately authoritarian control" (p. 138).

23. Roswitha Mattausch, *Siedlungsbau und Stadtneugründungen im deutschen Faschismus* (Frankfurt, 1981), p. 79.

24. Feder cited in Harlander, p. 60ff. and, Dieter Münk, "Die Organisation des Raumes im Nationalsozialismus," Ph.D. diss., University of Bonn, 1993, p. 181. See also Dirk Schubert, "Gottfried Feder und sein Beitrag zur Stadtplanungstheorie," *Die alte Stadt*, vol. 13 (1986), especially p. 204ff. Feder was not alone in his vision of small-town

Germany. In 1931, Rudolf Böhmer had created a stir with a book promoting the formation of *Ackerbürgerstädte* ("farmer-citizens' towns") with populations of not more than twelve thousand. Social Democrat and modernist Martin Wagner had also advanced, prior to 1933, a concept for medium-sized, decentralized, semirural cities of fifty thousand inhabitants. See Tilman Harlander, Katrin Hater, Franz Meiers, *Siedeln in der Not* (1988), pp. 57–58. The January 24, 1934, edition of the *Deutsche Bauzeitung* reported on a plan by C. Chr. Lörcher to establish a "network of hubs, small rural cities in regular intervals across the German empire" (p. 62). These were to be connected economically with their surrounding areas. The intellectual predecessor of all these ideas was, of course, Ebenezer Howard's original ideal of the garden city.

25. The orientation was the opposite of the subsistence homestead project insofar as the greenbelt communities explicitly concentrated on attractive real estate near cities rather than run-down inner-city or impoverished rural areas. Instead of trying to correct social imbalances between town and country, Tugwell's vision was a "more orderly pattern for the inevitable movement from farm to city," by which Tugwell actually meant not the city but the urban periphery. His ideas were ultimately less inspired by the garden-city ideal than the frontier movement of the nineteenth century, which aimed at settling ever more untouched stretches of nature, abandoning those that had previously been laid to waste. With the closing of the American frontier, attractive areas of land between town and country took over the role of territory to be "conquered." Yet, as was not the case with frontier expansion, the greenbelt communities were also intended to physically rejuvenate the urban spaces they surrounded. "My idea," Tugwell proclaimed, "is to go just outside centers of population, pick up cheap land, build a whole community and entice people into it. Then go back into the cities and tear down whole slums and make parks of them." Thus, with other means and goals, and in a completely different sense, the greenbelt communities also aimed at a kind of rural-urban symbiosis. Whereas the homesteads were intended to raise rural standards of living up to their urban equivalents, Tugwell's initiative hoped that subsidizing

promising areas would have a positive effect of "greening" run-down urban centers.

26. See Münk, p. 409.

27. Clemens J. Neumann, "Deutsches Siedeln und symbolisches Bauen," *Siedlung und Wirtschaft* (1934), p. 476.

28. Cited in Harlander, *Zwischen Heimstätte und Wohnmaschine*, p. 73.

Chapter 5. Public Works

1. Bernice Glatzer Rosenthal, *New Myth, New World* (University Park, 2002), and Rosenthal, editor, *Nietzsche and Soviet Culture* (Cambridge, Eng., 1994).

2. Hans Siemsen, *Russland: Ja und Nein* (Berlin, 1931), p. 147. See also Albert Rhys Williams, *The Soviets* (New York, 1937), p. 147.

3. Mario M. Morandi, "L'introduzione all'Agro Pontino," *Civiltà fascista*, vol. 2 (1935), pp. 1009–10.

4. Valentino Orsolini-Cencelli, "Littoria e la bonificazione dell'Agro Pontino," *Gerarchia* (1933), p. 850.

5. Another example of the relationship between individualism and collectivism in Fascist culture was the symbolic importance of machines and, in particular, motor vehicles. In his book *Staging Fascism*, cultural historian Jeffrey Schnapp investigates the role played in Fascist mythology by the 18BL truck. The 18BL was the Italian army's main transport vehicle in World War I, and as of 1919, it was also the vehicle of choice for Fascists, who used it to transport *squadri* to factory gates and party offices to do battle with the Italian socialists. After Mussolini came to power, it became a primary symbol of Fascist national renewal, one that was seen to combine man and machine, much in the fashion of racing cars and airplanes—with the important difference that it highlighted the collective, the group of Fascist fighters, over the individual "pilot." In a 1935 stage play, the 18BL even took over the role of hero originally intended for a nineteen-year-old

Fascist allegedly killed by socialists in the early days of Mussolini's movement. Schnapp writes, "The truck was the fascist everyman and everywoman, a humble and heroic soldier as well as soldier carrier, capable . . . of eliciting the same empathic reaction as the martyred body of Giovanni Berta." The 18BL, Schnapp concludes, was the "birth-mother of the revolution." *Staging Fascism: 18BL and the Theater of Masses for Masses* (Stanford, 1996), pp. 55, 56. Symbolically, the truck occupied an intermediary position between the railway as a mass and the automobile as an individual means of transport: "Trucks emerged as symbols of the collectivity early in modern transportation history because of their links . . . to industry and to the urban proletariat, on the one hand, and . . . to modernized agriculture and the peasantry on the other. Unlike in the case of trains, the collectivity in question cannot readily be identified with the state, *because of the exceptional degree of autonomy and freedom of movement granted by truck travel*" (p. 54; emphasis added).

6. On the term "anti-city," see Riccardo Mariani, "Monumentalismus und Monumente," in *Realismus: Zwischen Revolution und Reaktion* (Munich, 1981), p. 418. Architect Marcello Piacentini, a Mussolini mouthpiece, praised the amount of green space in the layout of the New Cities and their "organic" connection to their surrounding areas. At the same time he criticized their dimensions as overblown and their public amenities as underused. This led a later critic to complain that Piacentini "did not explain what he meant, and I have not yet found out what he may have had in mind." See Henry A. Millon, "Some New Towns in Italy in the 1930s," in *Art and Architecture in the Service of Politics*, edited by Millon and Linda Nochlin (Cambridge, Mass., 1978), pp. 332–33. Recognizing that the New Cities, despite their green spaces, were not intended to be garden cities proved difficult for both 1930s observers and later critics. Diane Ghirardo is likewise unclear about the relationship between the *nuova città* and the classical garden city, characterizing them alternately as fully distinct concepts (p. 60) and similar phenomena (p. 81; see chap. 4, n. 22).

7. McLeod, p. 308 (see chap. 4, n. 6).

8. Cited in Valentino Orsolini-Cencelli, "Littoria e la bonificazione dell'Agro Pontino," *Gerarchia* (1933), p. 851.

9. Corrado Alvaro, *Terra nuova: Prima cronaca dell'Agro Pontino* (1934; repr., Milan, 1989), pp. 15, 26, 29, 47–48, 78.

10. Cited in Schnapp, p. 57.

11. Ibid., p. 75.

12. Perhaps the reclamation of the Pontine Marshes can best be seen as an intermediary phenomenon, an expanded settlement to which the New Cities gave the external appearance of monumentality—that missing element which had made the settlement projects of the New Deal and National Socialism so ineffective as propaganda. It is instructive here to compare the Agro Pontino project with the forgotten "East Prussia plan" of the early Nazi regime.

The East Prussia plan was put forward in 1934 by party district head Erich Koch, who, like Gottfried Feder, was a member of the middle-class faction of the party. It aimed at reviving Germany's backwater, noncontiguous, easternmost territory. Koch's arguments for the project are familiar from the Agro Pontino. For Germany, East Prussia was the paradigm of a region that had been damaged by liberal industrialization. Demographically decimated by people moving west to work in the coal mines of the Ruhr Valley, it was reminiscent of a prairie frontier. Yet thanks to its geographic location, Koch also described East Prussia as "a vanguard, pathbreaking outpost for the German people on their way from the west to the east, from the big city to the land, from the tenement building to its native soil." Koch, *Aufbau im Osten* (Breslau, 1934), p. 65.

The scope of the East Prussia plan dwarfed that of its predecessor, the Eastern Relief initiative of the Weimar Republic, which had simply offered struggling landowners in the region financial assistance. Koch's plan proposed to increase the population from 2 to 3.5 million people by relocating small and medium-sized factories from western Germany and by turning industrial laborers into farmers. The enterprise was to have the double benefit of relieving urban crowding in western Germany and repopulating the "empty" east.

Another proponent of the plan, Heinz Schmalz, argued that resettlement in East Prussia would rejuvenate western German industry by allowing it "to find a new lease on life." Schmalz, *Die Industrialisierung Ostpreussens als Schicksalsfrage für den gesamtdeutschen und osteuropäischen Raum* (Berlin, 1934), p. 15. Schmalz imagined the new East Prussia as similar to Holland and the southwest German state of Württemberg, with their mixture of small- and medium-sized industrial and agricultural operations. He also saw the region as a bridgehead for Germany's colonial ambitions in Eastern Europe. The propaganda surrounding the plan in 1934 and 1935 contained all of these elements: the vision of recultivating a landscape ravaged by liberalism; the establishment of a middle-class mixed economy in which light industry and agriculture would harmoniously coexist; the realization of the *Landstadt* concept on nearly virgin soil; and the creation of a genuinely National Socialist form of culture from the wastelands of liberalism.

Significantly, the German Roosevelt biographer Helmut Magers saw a number of parallels between the East Prussia plan and the Tennessee Valley Authority. Magers, *Roosevelt*, pp. 110–11. For a short time, the project looked as though it could become the German equivalent of the Agro Pontino. But the initiative lacked the monumental elements necessary for propaganda value, and Koch's proposal was soon dropped in favor of constructing the autobahn.

13. Nonetheless, the plans Ford envisioned not only foreshadowed but went beyond those that would later be realized. As historian Walter L. Creese put it, "the balance, grandeur, and all-inclusive atmosphere of Ford's vision never truly would be equaled by the plans of later TVA thinkers." Creese, *TVA's Public Planning: The Vision, the Reality* (Knoxville, 1990), p. 29. On Ford and the Muscle Shoals project, see also Reynold M. Wik, *Henry Ford and Grass-Roots America* (Ann Arbor, 1972), pp. 112–13; David E. Nye, *Electrifying America: Social Meanings of a New Technology, 1880–1940* (Cambridge, Mass., 1990), p. 298; and Ronald Toby, *Technology as Freedom: The New Deal and the Electrical Modernization of the American Home* (Berkeley, 1996), pp. 48–49.

14. To an extent the TVA can be seen as a pilot project in a movement to divide the United States into administrative regions rather than according to the boundaries of the individual states. See William

E. Leuchtenburg, "Roosevelt, Norris and the 'Seven Little TVAs,'" *Journal of Politics*, vol. 14 (1954), p. 418, and Edward M. Barrows, "United Regions of America: A New American Nation," *New Outlook* (May 1933), p. 19ff.

15. Roosevelt cited in Schlesinger, *The Coming of the New Deal*, p. 324 (see chap. 2, n. 13). David Mitrany, *The Functional Theory of Politics* (New York, 1975), pp. 162–63. On the historical development and progressive idology of the public corporation, see Susan Tenenbaum, "The Progressive Legacy and the Public Corporation: Entrepreneurship and Public Virtue," *Journal of Policy History*, vol. 3 (1991), pp. 309–30.

16. David E. Lilienthal, *TVA: Democracy on the March* (New York, 1944), pp. 1–2.

17. Arthur E. Morgan, "The Human Problem of the Tennessee Valley Authority," *Landscape Architecture* (April 1934), p. 123. See also Donald Davidson, *The Tennessee*, vol. 2 (New York, 1948), p. 238.

18. "Totality": George Fort Milton, "Dawn for the Tennessee Valley," *Review of Reviews* (June 1933), p. 34. "Planning cannot": Julian Huxley, "An Achievement of Democratic Planning," *Architectural Review*, vol. 93 (1943), p. 166. Talbot F. Hamlin held a similar position: "There is also, I think, in the TVA project another, even deeper, source of hope and confidence. It is the world's most striking contemporary example that planning—large-scale planning—is possible in a democracy; that no such false efficiency as that of a dictatorship is necessary to produce great national works, conceived and executed for the benefit of all the people." Hamlin, "Architecture of the TVA," *Pencil Points*, vol. 20 (1939), p. 731. Today's estimations of the TVA are more ambivalent, as critics have come to realize that many of its achievements came about precisely because it was not democratic in structure. See, for example, Phoebe Cutler, *The Public Landscape of the New Deal* (New Haven, 1985), p. 136.

19. Cited in Schlesinger, *The Crisis of the Old Order, 1919–1933*, pp. 123–24 (see chap. 4, n. 8).

20. Emile Zola, *Travail* (Paris, 1993), p. 545–46. Author's translation.

21. James W. Carey and John J. Quirk, "The Mythos of the Electronic Revolution," *American Scholar* (Summer 1970), pp. 226–27. The idea of electricity as a source of salvation and regeneration has its roots in the so-called electrical theology of the eighteenth century, which saw God as the electrical source of all life. Franz Anton Mesmer's contemporaneous idea that the soul could be healed by "animal magnetism" can also be seen as a precursor to modern-day electroshock therapy.

22. Creese, pp. 54, 250.

23. F. A. Gutheim, "T.V.A.: A New Phase in Architecture," *Magazine of Art*, vol. 33 (September 1940), p. 527. In this context, one could also cite Lenin's idea of the dual dominion of two equally powerful classes temporarily balance each other out. The New Deal, which saw itself as an advocate of "the people" against rapacious capitalism, used its electrification program as both an economic weapon and a protective shield.

24. Cited in Creese, p. 162.

25. Brian Black, "Ecology and Design in the Landscape of the Tennessee Valley Authority, 1933–1945," in *Environmentalism in Landscape Architecture*, edited by Michael Conan (Washington, D.C., 2000), pp. 83–84.

26. Hamlin, p. 722.

27. See Creese, p. 165. One could also draw a comparison to the Metro in Moscow, which was publically inaugurated at roughly the same time as the Norris Dam. Although the technology in the Metro was concealed behind a pseudohistorical facade, the public-transport system in the Soviet capital was still celebrated as a revolutionary achievement in engineering. Although they came from opposite ends of the political spectrum, the American and Soviet governments converged insofar as they both initiated and propagandistically staged gigantic public works projects centered on new technology.

28. Gutheim, p. 524.

29. Hyacinthe Dubreuil, *Les codes de Roosevelt: Les perspectives de la vie sociale* (Paris, 1934), p. 136. To prove his point, Dubreuil cited Americans' minimal use of the horn and their strict observance of traffic lanes.

30. See Thomas Zeller, *Strasse, Bahn, Panorama: Verkehrswege und Landschaftsveränderung in Deutschland von 1930 bis 1990* (Frankfurt, 2002), p. 54. The idea of German technology can be seen as the National Socialist variant of the international technocratic movement of which Thorstein Veblen was the most prominent representative in the United States.

31. "The question": quoted in Erhard Schütz: "'Verankert fest im Kern des Bluts': Die Reichsautobahn—mediale Visionen einer organischen Moderne im 'Dritten Reich,'" in *Faszination des Organischen: Konjunkturen einer Kategorie der Moderne*, edited by H. Eggert, E. Schütz, and P. Sprengel (Munich, 1995), p. 236. That essay is nearly identical to Schütz, "Faszination der blassgrauen Bänder," in *Technikdiskurs der Hitler-Stalin-Ära*, edited by Wolfgang Emmerich and Carl Wege (Stuttgart, 1995). "Tightly drawn": quoted in Schütz, "Faszination," p. 128. "It was intended not to destroy": Hugo Koester (1943), cited in Zeller, p. 156. "Not the shortest": Emil Maier-Dorn (1938), cited in Schütz, "'Verankert,'" p. 240.

32. Karl-Heinz Ludwig, "Politische Lösungen für technische Innovatione 1933–1945," *Technikgeschichte*, vol. 62 (1995), p. 336.

33. Erhard Schütz and Eckhard Gruber, *Mythos Autobahn: Bau und Inszenierung der "Strassen des Führers," 1933–1941* (Berlin, 1996), p. 128.

34. Todt quoted in Zeller, *Strasse*, p. 83. See also Thomas Lekan, "Regionalism and the Politics of Landscape Preservation in the Third Reich," *Environmental History*, vol. 4 (1999), pp. 396–97.

35. Todt quoted in Thomas Zeller, "'The Landscape's Crown': Landscape, Perceptions, and Modernizing Effects of the German Autobahn System, 1934 to 1941," in *Technologies of Landscape: From Reaping to Recycling*, edited by David E. Nye (Amherst, 1999), p. 237. On comparisons between Todt and Taut, see Schütz, "'Verankert,'" p. 238.

36. For a bibliography of German publications on the American parkways, see Zeller, *Strasse*, p. 163.

37. Sigfried Giedion, *Space, Time and Architecture* (1941; repr., Cambridge, Mass., 1976), p. 825.

38. The phrase is Alvin Seifert's. Seifert was in charge of landscaping the autobahn and planning its course.

39. Walter Dirks, "Das Dreieck auf der Autobahn: Impressionen von einer Fahrt Frankfurt-Berlin-München-Frankfurt," *Frankfurter Zeitung*, December 11, 1938.

40. Schütz, "'Verankert,'" p. 259.

41. Stephen Henry Roberts, *The House That Hitler Built* (New York, 1938), p. 240.

42. See Carl Wege, "Gleisdreieck, Tank und Motor: Figuren und Denkfiguren aus der Technosphäre der Neuen Sachlichkeit," *Deutsche Vierteljahresschrift für Literaturwissenschaft und Geistesgeschichte*, vol. 68 (1994), pp. 320–23.

43. Joseph Roth, *What I Saw: Reports from Berlin, 1920–1933* (New York, 2003), pp. 105–08.

Epilogue: "As We Go Marching"

1. John T. Flynn, *As We Go Marching* (New York, 1944; repr., 1972), pp. 255, 256. Bertram Myron Gross, *Friendly Fascism: The New Face of Power in America* (New York, 1980).

2. Karl Mannheim, *Man and Society in an Age of Reconstruction* (New York, 1940), pp. 337–38.

Illustration Acknowledgments

akg-images: 53
© Alinari Archives, Florence: 147
Archiv der sozialen Demokratie der Friedrich-Ebert-Stiftung: 85
© Bettmann/CORBIS: 68
The Granger Collection, New York: 51, 155
Hulton Archive/Getty Images: 151
© Hulton-Deutsch Collection/CORBIS: 89
Library of Congress: 129, 130, 161
Mary Evans/Institute of Civil Engineers: 180
Mary Evans/Weimar Archive: 71, 175
Roger Viollet/Getty Images: 6
© SV-Bilderdienst/The Image Works: 133
© Topham/The Image Works: 58

Index

Page numbers in *italics* refer to illustrations.

About the Author

WOLFGANG SCHIVELBUSCH, who has been called "a master of cultural history," is an independent scholar who divides his time between New York and Berlin. His books include *The Culture of Defeat*, *The Railway Journey*, *Disenchanted Night*, and *Tastes of Paradise*.

About the Translator

JEFFERSON CHASE's translations include the Signet edition of Thomas Mann's *Death in Venice and Other Stories* and *The Culture of Defeat* by Wolfgang Schivelbusch. He lives in Berlin.